Not a Woman Architect
The Life and Work of
Brigitte Peterhans

Not a Woman Architect
The Life and Work of Brigitte Peterhans

Edited by David Fleener

Despite the hardships endured as a female architect during the *Mad Men* era, Brigitte Peterhans never felt that she was less privileged.
When a newspaper reporter called her and said, 'I understand you're one of the few women working at SOM.'
She responded, 'Talk to me as an architect, don't talk about women in architecture.' (1)

CONTENTS

PAGE
- 6   CARL SANDBURG'S 'CHICAGO'
- 8   CONTEXTUAL INTRODUCTORY ESSAY
- 14 INTRODUCTION
- 16 WORKING WITH BRIGITTE
- 18 MEMOIR BY JOHN VINCI
- 26 LIFE CHRONOLOGY
- 38 ARCHITECTURAL EDUCATION AT IIT
- 42 MASTER THESIS: STUDENTS' INTERNATIONAL HOUSE FOR THE UNIVERSITY OF CHICAGO
- 58 WORK AT SKIDMORE, OWINGS & MERRILL
- 116 WORK APART FROM SOM
- 158 APPENDIX 1: WALTER PETERHANS AND THE BAUHAUS
- 160 APPENDIX 2: DIARY OF AN OCEAN VOYAGE
- 186 ACKNOWLEDGEMENTS
- 186 ABBREVIATIONS
- 187 SOURCES
- 188 INDEX

Chicago

By Carl Sandburg

Source: *Poetry*, Poetry Foundation, 1914

          Hog Butcher for the World,
          Tool Maker, Stacker of Wheat,
          Player with Railroads and the Nation's Freight Handler,
          Stormy, husky, brawling,
          City of the Big Shoulders.

They tell me you are wicked and I believed them, for I have seen your painted women under the gas lamps luring the farm boys.
And they tell me you are crooked and I answer:
      Yes, it is true, I have seen the gunman kill and go free to kill again.
And they tell me you are brutal and my reply is:
      On the faces of women and children I have seen the marks of wanton hunger.
And having answered so I turn once more to those who sneer at this my city,
      and I give them back the sneer and say to them:
Come and show me another city with lifted head singing so proud to be alive
      and coarse and strong and cunning.
Flinging magnetic curses amid the toil of piling job on job,
      here is a tall bold slugger set vivid against the little soft cities;
Fierce as a dog with tongue lapping for action,
      cunning as a savage pitted against the wilderness,
          Bareheaded,
          Shoveling,
         Wrecking,
         Planning,
         Building, breaking, rebuilding,
Under the smoke, dust all over his mouth, laughing with white teeth,
Under the terrible burden of destiny laughing as a young man laughs,
Laughing even as an ignorant fighter laughs who has never lost a battle,
Bragging and laughing that under his wrist is the pulse,
      and under his ribs the heart of the people,
         Laughing!
Laughing the stormy, husky, brawling laughter of Youth,
      half-naked, sweating, proud to be Hog
      Butcher, Tool Maker, Stacker of Wheat,
      Player with Railroads and Freight Handler to the Nation.

CONTEXTUAL INTRODUCTORY ESSAY

The First School of Chicago Architecture: 1870–1910

Hog Butcher for the World, City of the Big Shoulders, yes, but also the birthplace and cradle of that most iconic of American building type, the skyscraper. After the Great Chicago Fire of 1871 razed over 17,000 buildings in the centre of the city, real estate speculators quickly began rebuilding it. But prior to the fire, as well as soon after it, Chicago, the fastest growing city in the world at that time, was already attracting architects from the East Coast to come and build its big shoulders. William Le Baron Jenney (came to Chicago in 1867) was the architect for the first all-steel frame building, the Home Insurance Building (1885–1931), considered the first skyscraper. This was in contrast to the masonry load-bearing walls used up to that time, which were limited in height due to the load-bearing capacity of brick and stone. The tallest load-bearing masonry building in the world is the Monadnock Building in Chicago, designed by Holabird and Root in 1891. At 16 storeys, its walls are six-feet thick at the base. Since being built, the building has sunk over 20 inches due to the weight of the masonry walls. It is also the first building in Chicago without a shred of ornament or historical reference.

Jenney was followed by Louis Sullivan (came to Chicago in 1873) – Auditorium Theater Building, Carson, Pirie, Scott and Company Store, Chicago Stock Exchange, Schiller Theater; Daniel Burnham (came to Chicago in 1867) – the Reliance Building, the Rookery, the Monadnock Building, Orchestra Hall, the Chicago Plan; William Holabird (came to Chicago in 1875) – the Marquette Building, the Monadnock Building southern half, the Chicago Building; and the German-born Dankmar Adler, a partner of Louis Sullivan. Altogether they formed the First School of Chicago Architecture. This school style is best defined by clearly expressed steel frame buildings with limited ornament. One distinctive feature of the school, the 'Chicago Window', is a large fixed-centre lite of glass with two smaller operable windows on either side; often these windows were extruded to form bay windows. The only Midwestern native architect practicing in Chicago at that time was Frank Lloyd Wright, whose individual Prairie Style was its own school of design.

Home Insurance Building, Chicago, under construction, 1885, William Le Baron Jenney

The first all-steel frame high-rise building.

Chapter—Introduction

Monadnock Building, Chicago, 1891, Burnham and Root _ David K. Staub, photographer

At 16 storeys, the world's tallest building with masonry-bearing walls.
Note the lack of ornament or historical reference.

The Chicago Building, Chicago, 1904, Holabird and Roche _ Chicago Designslinger

The 'Chicago Window' both flat and in bay form.

The Link Between Chicago and Germany

In 1911, Berlin publisher Ernst Wasmuth published a portfolio of the work of Chicago architect Frank Lloyd Wright with elaborate plan and perspective drawings. The influence of this work on European architects was immense. The Austrian architects Richard Neutra and Rudolf Schindler were inspired to move to the United States seeking to work for Wright. The publication was also accompanied by an exhibition, attended by the German architect Mies van der Rohe, who later wrote: 'The more we were absorbed in the study of these creations, the greater became our admiration for [Wright's] incomparable talent, the boldness of his conceptions and the independence of his thought and action. The dynamic impulse emanating from his work invigorated a whole generation. His influence was strongly felt even when it was not actually visible.' (Philip Johnson, *Mies van der Rohe* (New York: Museum of Modern Art, 1947))

In 1930 and 1931, the American architectural historian Russell Hitchcock, critic Philip Johnson, and the New York Museum of Modern Art director Alfred Barr Jr., toured Europe to see contemporary architecture. After returning to New York, in 1932 they curated an exhibition of this work entitled *Modern Architecture: International Exhibition,* which coined the term 'International Style'. After this exhibition, Hitchcock and Johnson 'travelled to Chicago in search of local sources for the international style, sources that predated and perhaps influenced its appearance in Europe. The material they gathered became the basis for the MoMA's second architecture exhibition, *Early Modern Architecture: Chicago 1870–1910*'. (Joanna Merwood-Salisbury, 'American Modern: The Chicago School and the International Style at New York's Museum of Modern Art', as published in Alexander Eisenschmidt and Jonathan Mekinda, *Chicagoisms: The City as Catalyst for Architectural Speculation*, (Zurich: Park Books, 2013))

The Second School of Chicago Architecture: 1940–1980
The Second School of Chicago Architecture began in 1938 when German architect Mies van der Rohe came to Chicago. Mies had been the director of the German Bauhaus school of design, which had been shut down by the Nazis. Initially, Mies was offered a position at Harvard University's Graduate School of Design. He decided instead to come to Chicago's Armour Institute of Technology, later the Illinois Institute of Technology (IIT.) As part of the deal he struck with IIT, he was given rein to overhaul the architectural curriculum, and he asked two other Bauhaus teachers to join him: city planner and architect Ludwig Hilbersheimer, and photographer Walter Peterhans. Another part of the deal was the ability to design a new campus on Chicago's South Side. It was with these classroom buildings that Mies began to develop the architectural language he would pursue for the rest of his life, and that became the core of the new curriculum – the tectonic expression of structure and the honest use of materials.

Although Mies, his students, and his followers designed many iconic low-rise buildings, as in the First School of Chicago Architecture, it was the skyscraper that epitomised the Second School. Following Mies' groundbreaking 860–880 Lake Shore Drive Apartments, larger architectural firms contributed to defining this school – Skidmore, Owings & Merrill's Inland Steel Building, Hancock Center, and Sears Tower; and Jacque Brownson of C.F. Murphy's Civic Center (now the Daley Center).

It is not known if Mies was attracted to Chicago because of its architectural heritage, most likely it was merely the offer from the Armour Institute of Technology. Similarly, it was not the heritage of the Chicago School of Architecture that attracted Brigitte Peterhans to come to Chicago, rather it was the encouragement of Mies' *protégé* Myron Goldsmith who accidentally met her in Germany, showed her photos of the Farnsworth House that he had been assisting Mies with, and suggested Brigitte attend the Illinois Institute of Technology where Mies was still teaching. Nevertheless, the buildings of the First School of Chicago Architecture had a profound impact on the development of the Second School led by Mies and his followers.

INTRODUCTION

It was a bright spring day that filled the vast universal space of Crown Hall with sunlight.[a] I was a student sitting at my desk when out of the corner of my eye I espied a striking woman with a black bob haircut step right out of an Otto Dix painting.[b] Unbeknownst to me and unbelievable at that time, five years later I would be working for her in the architectural offices of Skidmore, Owings & Merrill (SOM), and we would remain close for the next 40 years, until she died. To those in the know, Mies van der Rohe, Ludwig Hilbersheimer, and Walter Peterhans were legends at IIT, having moved to Chicago from the Bauhaus in Germany, in 1938, to establish the new architectural curriculum, still being taught there when I was a student in the 1970s. While the three of them were long gone, just seeing the widow of one of them was a link to the past, and a heartthrob at that.

I started at SOM in 1977 working on the Hajj Terminal of the King Abdul Azziz International Airport in Jedda, Saudi Arabia. When that project wound down, I was transferred to a different studio to work on the design of the new SOM offices to be located at 33 West Monroe in Chicago. Brigitte Peterhans was the senior designer on that project, but she was away visiting her sick mother in Germany the first few weeks I was there. When she returned, a co-worker told her that I had been born in Munich, Germany, and that I played the piano, and that sealed it. I became the apple of her eye. Not having children of her own, she became my surrogate mother, mentoring, chastising, feeding, clothing, promoting, criticising, beseeching, and all the things a mother does. The fact that I was born to a German mother with no known father, and then adopted by Americans and raised in Missouri, fascinated Brigitte. She always had theories about who my natural father was, usually it was a Catholic priest. She often noted that Cardinal Ratzinger (later Pope Benedict) was archbishop of Munich when I was born, but when I pointed out that she herself was working in Munich at the time, the theorising halted, at least temporarily. In spite of that, she insisted on accompanying me to my hometown, Chillicothe, Missouri, to meet my adopted parents, to attend the church I grew up in, and to see the schools I went to. In 1987, I left SOM to go work for the architect Dirk Lohan, the grandson of Mies, and Brigitte had left Chicago to work in the London office of SOM. After retiring from SOM, Brigitte went to Stuttgart in Germany to design a house for her brother

Jörg Schlaich. In 2000, I started my own practice, and Brigitte returned to Chicago. Although she consulted with me on projects at my firm, our relationship became less professional and more friends and family. We travelled together throughout the US, Europe, and Egypt. We hiked the Indiana dunes, and we swam in Lake Michigan. I helped entertain, and became close friends with, many of her nieces and nephews who visited from Germany. So many of my closest friends and I met through Brigitte, including John Vinci, Sonia Cooke, Ani Afshar, and Ursula Sobek.

Brigitte Peterhans was an architecture student and professional architect at a time when the field was dominated by men, and in the time of *Mad Men*.[c] Like the few other women architects at that time, she did not achieve the fame and notoriety of her male peers in spite of being their equal, if not superior, in terms of design ability and construction knowledge. Additionally, like Mies, she was not interested in associating with a political entity, like many other female architects of that time, such as Margarete Schütte-Lihotzky. Thus, whether it was her German cultural roots or her distinctive personality, she never considered herself a 'woman' architect, but only an architect.

The women architects of Brigitte's era, those born before 1940, 'struggled both to be allowed entry into the architectural profession and to be recognised for their work.'(8) As noted in the frontispiece to this book, Brigitte refused to consider herself a 'woman' architect. This was partially due to a lack of ambition, which prevented her from achieving the notoriety of some of her female contemporaries. She had no interest in joining the Chicago Women in Architecture club, which had been founded by her friends and cohorts at SOM, Natalie de Blois, and Nancy Abshire (another founding member was Gertrude Kerbis, a previous wife of Peterhans). Rather, she was generous with her time and support of SOM female non-architectural staff, remaining lifelong friends with Bruce Graham's assistant, Sonia Cooke. She often organised lunchtime extracurricular activities for them, such as watercolour painting classes.

a) IIT College of Architecture, designed by Mies van der Rohe, Chicago, 1955
b) German Expressionist artist (1891–1969)
c) American television drama set from 1960 to 1970

WORKING WITH BRIGITTE

By studying under Mies, Brigitte learned early on that initial design ideas are rarely cohesive and require intensive further investigation. This realisation, combined with periods of self-doubt, would often make working on architectural problems time-consuming and even, on occasion, tedious for both Brigitte and her design team. Work often entailed all-night charettes as milestone deadlines loomed. Although she was a good mentor, she expected a certain foundation of architectural knowledge from her co-workers, and would not tolerate incompetence. If you could not draw an accurate straight line, or add two-plus-two, you would be out on your ear. Being an *echt* German, she never hesitated to vocalise her opinions or demands. More than once, when a co-worker demonstrated incompetence, I would hear her yell out loud from her desk to the project manager 'Tomlinson, get rid of that boy!' Even within earshot of said boy.
SOM was a large firm, with many complex projects, and architects were assigned one of three specific roles – design, technical, or project management. Brigitte had little tolerance for so-called designers, architects with little or no basis in the technical aspects of architecture. In addition to being primarily a designer herself, she oversaw the technical production of her projects as well, including insisting on signing-off on all shop drawing reviews. While she held respect for those architects who specialised in the technical side, she had little respect for so-called project managers. One of the general partners in Chicago SOM was a managing/finance partner. Brigitte always kept some loose coins in her ash tray (she didn't smoke, but in those days almost everyone had an ashtray), and when she saw the finance partner coming, she would rattle the coins in her hand, especially if she knew he could hear it.
Brigitte was especially demanding of female architects, harbouring a perhaps misguided assumption that they were not technically proficient, and she was particularly dismissive of interior designers who had no architectural training. She could, by her criticism, reduce even the manliest of architects to tears or violent illness. And yet those who learned from her never forgot how and from whom they became better architects.

All was not sombre, and a jocular attitude often pervaded the atmosphere. In my time, it was customary to always take advantage of April Fool's Day. One year a friend and I brought 'invisible ink' to the studio. It came in a small plastic bottle. When squirted on material, a blue ink spot would appear, but after a few moments it would disappear. That year, I sat down beside Brigitte at her desk and complimented her on the silk blouse she was wearing. She replied, 'This old rag?' I then squirted her with the invisible ink and all of a sudden it was a 500 dollar blouse, how dare I? Then she said, 'Give me that bottle of ink'. We all went back to work at our stations. Later that day, Bruce Graham visited the studio and Brigitte went up to him with the bottle of ink and tried to squeeze it on his white shirt. None of the ink came out at first so she squeezed really hard and emptied the entire bottle on his shirt. In the studio we were all 'elbows down and asses up' while concealing our snickering. Bruce replied that if it didn't disappear, he would make her eat his shirt!

MEMOIR
John Vinci, Architect and Friend

After many years of friendship and shared experiences, I warmly remember Brigitte Peterhans as a determined and compassionate person, melded with an honest edge of directness. As an architect and designer, she was a person of many gifts.
I was a 20-year-old sophomore studying architecture at Illinois Institute of Technology (IIT) in 1957 when Brigitte Schlaich arrived at the school from Germany. Like many at IIT, she was motivated by the opportunity to study architecture under Mies van der Rohe. Brigitte was nine years older than me and arrived with experience gained from her schooling in Germany. But to qualify for the graduate program, the school's policies required her to start in the undergraduate classes. Brigitte first appeared in my construction class, which was taught by Professor Alfred Caldwell. His class required strict discipline and a large amount of drawing. Proving to ever-exacting Caldwell that she had extensive experience in architectural detailing from her previous schooling, Brigitte succeeded in entering the graduate program the following semester.
In 1958, Brigitte married the distinguished IIT professor Walter Peterhans, a gifted artist and photographer who had taught with Mies at the Bauhaus. The same year, IIT announced that Mies van der Rohe was retiring as director of the School of Architecture. The school also announced that Mies had resigned from his dual position as campus architect. His replacement, the school said, would be the firm Skidmore, Owings & Merrill. We, the members of AIA's student organisation, thought this sounded suspicious. Our understanding was that Mies very much wanted to stay on as campus architect. So, we held a meeting and began an inquiry. Upon hearing this, Brigitte invited us to her apartment where Walter Peterhans shared a copy of Mies' resignation letter in which he specifically stated he planned to continue serving as campus architect. Our next step was to visit William Hartman, President of Skidmore, Owings & Merrill, to protest. This was to no avail and ended our attempts to retain Mies as the campus architect. Through this and other school activities, I came to know Brigitte fairly well. When I received a fellowship to work in Milan during the summer of 1959, an invitation came from Brigitte to visit her and Peterhans during their stay in Germany, an invitation which I regrettably was not able to accept.

A major change in Brigitte's life came in 1960 when Walter died during a visit to her family's home in Germany. Brigitte returned to Chicago, where she worked at Skidmore, Owings & Merrill while completing her studies at IIT. It was a firm where she remained for most of her professional life. My own studies at IIT were completed in 1960, and I was now the owner of a Fiat 600. Brigitte asked me to teach her how to drive. She was difficult at first, wanting only to learn the basic steps, but she caught on very quickly. Anyone who ever drove with Brigitte will remember it as a precarious experience, yet she drove for most of her life in countries throughout Europe, Africa, and Asia, and to my knowledge she never had a serious accident.

Brigitte often had visitors, many of whom were family members. During one visit, the family of her brother Jörg had their child Michael baptised at the Mies' Saint Savior's Chapel on the IIT campus, and I attended the ceremony. Familial connections remained with the children of Walter Peterhans' previous marriages. Nini and Michael were from his first marriage to Gesine Weise. Julian was the son from his marriage to Gertrude Lempp. I came to know them through their visits or during my own travels. Nini came to Chicago to study at IIT's Institute of Design, and briefly lived with Brigitte. Just as I had done for Brigitte years earlier, I taught Nini to drive. Julian looked very much like his father, which I think was comforting to Brigitte. He was very interested in learning about the father he never really knew. Over the years, I drove Brigitte's mother, aunts, nephews, and nieces on various excursions around Chicago. Brigitte's mother came to visit in the early 1960s, at which time I invited her to my parents' house for dinner. Though neither my mother nor Brigitte's mother spoke English, they warmly bonded. Brigitte often told me how her mother fondly remembered the occasion. My parents' home at 5427 South Komensky was my first executed design, and Brigitte visited there on several occasions. Brigitte particularly admired a Tiffany Turtle-Back lamp that was one of my first acquisitions. She once offered to marry me for the lamp.

At one point in our relationship, Brigitte offered me a job to go work with her in Germany. I had to think about it, but ultimately turned it down. I was enjoying my current position in the office of Brenner Danforth Rockwell, and the need to learn German seemed too much of a challenge. In my place, I recommended my good friend David Norris, who accepted the offer and remained there for several years.

After the death of Peterhans, Brigitte worked to realise several of his uncompleted projects. In 1963, she undertook organising his collection of Visual Training plates created with his students at IIT. The goal was to have them all photographed for a book representing Walter Peterhans' students' best work. She was then living in a rooming house on East Erie Street and parking her Volkswagen on the street. One night, she left what we referred to as the 'Peterhans Plates' in her car. Thieves broke into the car, and the plates were gone. Brigitte enlisted my to help recover the irreplaceable lost materials. My friend Edward T. Hall, a noted anthropologist, suggested contacting the local alderman's office. His thinking was that since most elected officials in Chicago have ties to the criminal underworld, recovering them shouldn't be that difficult. Upon inquiry, however, Alderman Mayer Goldberg curtly replied that nothing could be done. The loss was devastating. Despite it, Brigitte still retained some of Walter Peterhans' photographic negatives and some excellently printed original images. Brigitte asked my advice on who could make prints of similar quality from the negatives, and I introduced her to my friend Richard Nickel. After much experimentation, Richard realised that the vibrancy of the existing prints derived significantly from the photographic papers they were printed on, and these papers were now out of production. Brigitte listened intently and ultimately selected a potentially promising contemporary paper. Even with the best efforts, we all found the resulting prints disappointing. In her next attempt to secure satisfactory prints from the Peterhans negatives, Brigitte turned to Gunther Sander, the son and former assistant to the noted German photographer August Sander. Gunther Sander was renowned as a master of photographic printing and produced some beautiful prints at his studio in Cologne. But something went awry in their relationship and Brigitte lost control of the project. In the end, only a few of the photographs were printed and Brigitte never got the negatives back.

Brigitte often displayed remarkable acts of generosity and compassion. She was known to check in on lonely elderly neighbours in need of company and assistance. In one memorable example, she became concerned about the welfare of eccentric artist Lee Godie, who sold her paintings on the street and sometimes on the steps of the Art Institute of Chicago where she proclaimed her offerings to be the real art. By night, she often slept in the public parks. Brigitte offered Godie access to her apartment for showers and respite, but the reclusive artist only did so on a couple of occasions. Whenever Brigitte encountered Godie on the street, she paid generously for her paintings, along with offers of food and assistance. Godie is now highly regarded by Chicago's art community. Fulfilling her proclamations on the Art Institute steps, Lee Godie's paintings are now included in the museum's collections, including one that she gave to me. Another titled 'The Architect' was drawn especially for Brigitte, however, it portrayed a man sporting a moustache.

Brigitte was fascinated by music of all kinds. She was a frequent companion for opera performances, and in later years attended simulcasts with us of New York's Metropolitan Opera at local movie theatres. She was also an engaged companion at the Chicago Symphony, offering perceptive critiques of the music and the conductors. Back in our student days at IIT, our musical expeditions were of an entirely different kind. Because I had a car, we went to see the live acts for many of Chicago South Side's legendary performers at clubs and nightspots visited by primarily Black audiences. Two memorable examples we witnessed were the powerful Delta Blues legend, Muddy Waters, and the great Jazz saxophone master, John Coltrane.

The South Side had theatres that offered live acts in combination with movies. At the Tivoli we saw the Four Tops, paired with the great Sarah Vaughn. The audience was primarily there to see the Four Tops, the slickly dressed popular vocalists who performed with highly synchronised sound and motion. Sarah Vaughn was largely ignored by the audience. She was in her last years and at the time was singing Brazilian inspired music, but her voice was in excellent shape. At the end of the performance Brigitte said to me, 'I'm not sure what to think – her voice is like a musical instrument.'

Singer Nina Simone was one of Brigitte's favourites. We sought out her performances at places like the Sutherland Hotel and a newly opened live performance bar in the Lake Meadows shopping centre. In the fall of 1961, Brigitte gathered a group of friends to see Simone perform at the Roberts Show Lounge, and on that visit unexpectedly became part of the performance herself. Simone was known for wanting silence and respectful attention while performing and would abruptly storm off the

stage if the proper decorum was not provided. As our group sat respectfully at one of the club's large round tables, all went well until a noisy group entered during her second number. She angrily admonished the group and the audience in general, lashing out with, 'You people just can't sit still. From now on, you can only hear me in a concert if you behave yourselves.' Simone then walked off the stage, and in a spontaneous reaction, Brigitte got out of her chair and followed the angry entertainer into her dressing room. Simone didn't seem perturbed by her unexpected visitor, muttering as she changed into her street clothes, 'I don't want to go out there anymore. They might as well listen to the radio. They might as well listen to the jukebox.'
Brigitte countered her with 'You're fabulous!' And she tried to convince Simone to finish her performance. 'You seem to be European,' commented the entertainer.
'Yes. I'm German,' responded Brigitte. After a polite exchange and thank you, Nina Simone returned to the stage and performed a few more songs.
In 1970, I purchased a house in Chicago at 3152 North Cambridge. With her extensive travels and geographically diverse projects, Brigitte was often transient in her living accommodations. My home often became her temporary quarters until she found a new apartment. She often called my place on Cambridge her second home. By the late 1970s, throughout the 1980s, and 1990s Brigitte was given more responsibilities at Skidmore, Owings & Merrill. She had projects in London, Egypt, and Spain among other far-ranging places. We corresponded during her travels, and she stayed at my house during brief returns to Chicago. Travel constituted a significant part of my time with Brigitte. She was always enthusiastic for travel opportunities, and adventuresome in seeking out places of interest. Although an excellent travel companion, the time together wasn't without occasional uncomfortable moments. Brigitte was not hesitant to express displeasure when accommodations or services did not meet her expectations, and there were sometimes surprises when she would abruptly insist on a change of plans. A memorable early trip together came in 1971, when I had the opportunity to meet Brigitte's father in France. It was planned that we would all meet at Chartres Cathedral. Upon arrival at the designated location, I found her father sitting on a bench waiting for me. He was a Lutheran pastor, and I was immediately put at ease by his kind face. Brigitte spoke of him often and told of how

he had run a hospital for 'indigent' children. She said that during the war it became clear that Hitler was disposing of such children. At great risk, her father planned for their safe relocation. Brigitte recalled seeing those left behind picked up by buses with whitewashed windows, then taken to concentration camps.

Another special trip came in 1972, shortly after the death of photographer Richard Nickel. Nickel was a mutual friend who was killed in a collapse while documenting the demolition of the Chicago Stock Exchange Building, a notable 1894 work by architects Adler and Sullivan. Brigitte and I planned a trip to visit one of Richard's most influential mentors, photographer Frederick Sommer, who lived with his wife Francis in a modest house in a wooded area of Prescott, Arizona. We drove through the desert, saw the Grand Canyon, and visited Paolo Soleri's utopian city Arcosante.

The spontaneity of our travels was demonstrated by a 1998 visit to India. Architectural historian Paul Sprague told me about a tour of India he was organising for the Walter Burley Griffin Society, an organisation devoted to preserving the legacy of the early twentieth century 'Prairie School' architect who had practiced in Chicago, Australia, and finally in India. The trip was in jeopardy due to not having enough participants. Although last minute and totally unexpected, the trip sounded appealing. It appealed to Brigitte too and also to my Detroit-based client Susan Hilberry. With the quota successfully reached, off we went. As a prelude, we first visited Dhaka, Bangladesh, where we toured the architecture of Louis Kahn. The itinerary for the Griffin Society included stops in Nepal, Bhubaneshwar, Calcutta, New Delhi, Agra, Chandigarh, and finally Lucknow, where Griffin planned his last buildings. Brigitte provided some unexpected challenges when she would stray from the tour group, and on one occasion tried to rearrange our accommodations. Although it momentarily generated consternation among the group, the incidents were largely forgotten as the tour progressed.

An ambitiously planned trip to China came in 2012. It was an extended journey meticulously worked out with architect Robert Turner, one of Brigitte's SOM colleagues who was also a friend of mine. First stop on the itinerary was Hong Kong, where we were joined by David Norris, a long-time friend going back to our student days at IIT. Since David had been working in Hong Kong, we anticipated that he could be helpful in navigating the language challenges. To our surprise, his regional Mandarin was incompatible with most of the places we visited. The trip coincided with my invitation to visit Weishan, a small Chinese city on the Silk Road near the border with Vietnam, which was undergoing restoration. Since I was known as a restoration architect, we were welcomed as honoured guests. For the next step of our journey, Turner planned for us to take a boat down the Li River on a one-day journey. The trip went smoothly, but complications arose when our connecting flight was delayed for hours with conflicting information suggesting it might be cancelled altogether. We hired a taxi to drive us about 100 miles to the port where our ship was to depart for Shanghai. It was a close call, with only a half hour to spare. Once aboard the ship, it was a pleasant three-day journey, with Turner arranging for accommodations in a major suite just above the ship's prow. We navigating a series of locks, and arrived in Shanghai on a rainy evening. A major Shanghai destination was SOM's Jin Mao Tower, where we explored the skyscraper and its impressive interiors. Another major tower by architect Ieoh Ming Pei was still under construction. From Shanghai to Beijing, our journey became a driving trip, passing through several towns with impressive pagodas. Instead of going to the local zoo, we opted for an alternative zoo in a wooded mountain area. As the trip was winding down, I experienced some uncomfortable scrimmages with Brigitte. It almost seemed as if she was playing favourites between David and I. When I think about it now, I realise that she was reunited among her favourite male friends going back to her first arrival in Chicago. Brigitte was sad the trip would be ending, and realised David would be departing our group early to resume his job in Hong Kong. In the end, we appreciated the experience together as a memorable and grand reunion among old friends. For all, it was a trip worth taking. Another warmly remembered trip was a car journey with Brigitte and David Fleener to the home of Robert Turner, the travel companion on our 2012 trip to China. On our way, we spent the night at the restored Shaker Village at Pleasant Hill, Kentucky, then on to Turner's beautiful modernist enclave of his own design near Blacksburg, Virginia. The visit also included a stop at the nearby campus of Virginia Polytechnic Institute where Turner, along with other SOM architects, had once gone to school.

On the drive back we experienced along the way scenic Appalachian landscapes and a memorable drive over the extraordinary New River Gorge Bridge, a dramatic West Virginia arched span rendered in Cor-Ten steel. We made a stop in Cincinnati to visit Zaha Hadid's Contemporary Arts Center museum, a brief stop in Cleveland, and then finally returned to Chicago.

On a 2003 vacation accompanied by Bruce Baker, we travelled to meet Brigitte in Berlin, then went to Lithuania to meet with our artist friend Kozis Varnelis. He had left Lithuania after the communists occupied the country, and relocated to Chicago. Brigitte had bought one of his paintings for the interior she had designed for SOM's apartment to house visiting guests in the John Hancock Center. Kozis was a strong advocate of his native country and managed to assemble significant works, such as books, maps, and memorabilia of national importance. Lithuania welcomed him back and honoured him with a museum for his collection and paintings. We were able to see each other for one last time.

Brigitte's last years coincided with the isolation resulting from the COVID-19 epidemic. Major long-distance public travel was out of the question, but a compact little group consisting of Brigitte, David Fleener and myself improvised our own Sunday automobile trips to see architecture and cultural sites throughout the Chicago area. They included visits to obscure South Side buildings designed by familiar mid-century modernists, like Paul Schweikher and Jacques Brownson. Brigitte Peterhans' last major trip was a solo journey to Germany. It was on this trip that she came down with a fatal sickness and passed away amidst the company of her family. From long experience and friendship, I knew the methodical preciseness she applied to everything she undertook. It seemed like a perfectly planned ending to a remarkable life and a very special friendship.

LIFE CHRONOLOGY

The first recorded Schlaich was Johann Schlaich (Schleich), father of Michael Schlaich (1635–1695), a preacher in Lindau, Germany, and forerunner of several generations of Lutheran pastors, including Brigitte's father Ludwig Schlaich, and her brother Peter Schlaich.

1928 Eva Brigitte Schlaich (she later changed her name to Brigitte Eva) was born in Sulz am Neckar, Germany, on 27 August, to Ludwig Schlaich and Elisabeth Weiss Schlaich. Her father was born in 1899 in Jaffa, Palestine, where his parents, Albert Eugen Schlaich and Julie Schlaich, nee Gößler, were living for some time in a complex owned by Plato von Ustinov, Peter Ustinov's grandfather. Albert Schlaich was a pastor of the Lutheran Church and worked for the 'Jerusalem Verein'. Although Albert correctly identified the financial misconduct of a fellow resident, he was nevertheless accused of betrayal and expelled from the community. In 1906, the family returned to Rutisheim, Germany, where Albert was the local pastor of the Lutheran Church. Later, her father Ludwig completed a theology degree in religion at Tübingen University. He wanted to be a missionary in China and trained in England in 1923 to be a missionary. At this time, he became a 'religious socialist'. Her mother wanted to be a doctor but, due to unfortunate circumstances, she became a nurse at a Stuttgart hospital until her children were born.

1930 Brigitte and her parents moved to Stetten, near Stuttgart, where her father became the theological leader and pastor of the 'Heil und Pflegeanstalt Stetten' (today the Diakonie Stetten), a home, school, and workshop for people of all ages with mental disabilities or epilepsy.

1931 Brigitte's brother Peter Schlaich was born in Stetten. Peter married Dorothy Laiblin (1930–2013) and took over from his father as director and pastor at the Diakonie. They have four sons: Florian, Sebastian, Nikolaus, and Kilian. Florian studied physics and is an IT consultant, Sebastian was a doctor (d. 2019), Nikolaus is a biologist, and Kilian is an IT consultant.

1934   Brigitte's brother Jörg Schlaich was born in Kernen-Stetten (d. 2021). Jörg married fashion designer Eve Fezer (1937–). Jörg worked as chief engineer under structural engineer Fritz Leonhardt with the architects Günter Behnisch and Frei Otto on the 1972 Munich Olympics cable net roof structured stadiums. He formed his own structural engineering firm Schlaich Bergermann Partner in Stuttgart in 1980. In 2010, he moved with Eve to Berlin to be near their four children: Mike, Frieder, Sibylle, and Anne. Mike Schlaich replaced his father as one of the heads of the firm upon his father's retirement. Frieder is a film producer, Sibylle is a graphic designer, and Anne is a set designer.

1934   Brigitte began her schooling at the Volksschule Stetten.

1936   Brigitte's brother Konrad Schlaich was born in Stetten (d. 1979). Konrad married Edith (1937–). Konrad worked as a mechanical/industrial engineer in Darmstadt. They have two children: Clara, and Hans-Jacob. Clara is a physician in Hamburg, and Hans-Jacob is a physicist at the European Central Bank in Frankfurt.

1937   Brigitte's brother Klaus Schlaich was born in Stetten (d. 2005). Klaus married Katrin Grimm and worked as a professor of law at the University of Bonn. They have three sons: Sönke, Christoph, and Johannes. Sönke is a lawyer in Madrid, Christoph is an architect in Cologne, and Johannes is a professor of mobility and transport at Berliner Hochschule für Technik.

1938   Brigitte became a member, and later an officer, of the League of German Girls (BDM), the female equivalent of the all-male Hitler Youth, which was compulsory for all young girls at that time. Brigitte and her siblings all studied a musical instrument at home, Brigitte studied the piano with her father. The family also practiced chorale singing every day at home. Brigitte continued her schooling at the Girls Gymnasium in Bad Cannstatt.

1933 – During the terrible times of Nazi Germany (1933–1945) more than
1945 300 residents with disabilities at the Anstalt Stetten were murdered by the Nazi regime as part of the 'euthanasia program for worthless life'. Pastor Ludwig Schlaich resisted the Nazi regime as much as he could and tried to save every life. As a result of his resistance, the Nazis closed down Ludwig Schlaich's Anstalt in 1940. It was reopened after the war. After the closure, the family moved to Heilbronn where Brigitte's grandparents lived. Brigitte's father Ludwig became a lieutenant in the German army, stationed at Bietigheim-Bissingen in occupied France. In 1941, Ludwig was transferred to the logistics division of the army and stationed in Ukraine. That year he was injured in the arm and spent three years recovering in hospitals in Germany. In 1944, he was sent to Italy until the end of Second World War, and returned home after three months as a prisoner under the Americans.

1944 Heilbronn was destroyed by an air raid. The Schlaich family took refuge in their cellar. When a bomb hit the street outside Brigitte's grandparents' home, it caused a stone to covered the escape hatch of the cellar. The only other exit from the cellar was a stairway that was on fire. Brigitte knew that continued fire would deplete the cellar of oxygen, so she took an axe and broke through the metal security screen on the escape hatch window, pushed the stone away, and led the family to safety. After the bombing the family went to a cousin's house in Bernloch. Finally in 1946, the family returned to the Stetten Diakonie.

1945 Brigitte attended a boarding school at a monastery named Urspring near Ulm.

1947 Brigitte's father encouraged her to get a college degree as marriage was unlikely due to the few eligible bachelors remaining after the war. When she applied to the university, she was asked if she had completed her *Abitur* ('high school diploma'), the interviewer doubted her age because she wore two-foot-long braids. She went home and cut off her braids and went back wearing makeup for the first and last time in her life. She entered the University of Stuttgart wanting to study interior design but was persuaded by Professor Adolph Schneck to study architecture first. He said you have to study architecture to be a really good interior designer. Entry requirements included working for half a year on the physical reconstruction of the bombed university buildings. There were no studio rooms for drafting and model building, only rooms for lectures, so Brigitte commuted the 10 miles to school in Stuttgart from Stetten by bicycle, doing her course work at home while living at home to help her sickly mother with housework. Architectural history at the university ranged from Egyptian to Greek, and Roman. Any history after that time contained German history, and which had been 'Nazified', and all the Nazi books had been destroyed after the war.

1949   Brigitte spent the summer vacation working as a farmhand in the Swiss Bernese Oberland. The family was poor and the work on the farm was physically demanding. Among her many tasks was taking milk on a horse and buggy to a cheese-making plant.

1950   Brigitte spent her summer vacation traveling alone along the Rhine River visiting famous cathedrals and castles. While staying in a hostel in Zurich she met Chicago architect Myron Goldsmith who was traveling to Germany from Italy on a bicycle, after studying with structural engineer Pier Luigi Nervi on a Fulbright scholarship. Myron had broken his arm and Brigitte offered to iron his shirt for him. Myron asked her what she was studying and when she said architecture, he showed Brigitte photographic slides of the steel structure of Mies' Farnsworth House which he had worked on. Myron encouraged her to apply for a Fulbright scholarship and go to IIT to study with Mies. German knowledge of contemporary developments in architecture was scarce in Germany at that time, so Myron continued to send Brigitte magazines and articles about Mies, SOM, Frank Lloyd Wright.

1951   Brigitte inherited an interest in Muslim culture and architecture from her father who had spent his childhood in Palestine. She spent this summer working on a North Atlantic Treaty Organization (NATO) road project, building gas stations and rest houses in Ankara, Turkey. These roads were being built to the Black Sea to prepare Turkey in case of war with Russia. She also found time to travel alone through Yugoslavia.

1954   Brigitte failed at her first attempt at a Fulbright scholarship when the interviewer asked her if she had read any American fiction such as Faulkner and she said she hadn't. She returned home and read some American fiction. Of the second interview she said, 'I really knew how to do it. If I had no answer, I just made one up. All you had to do is be aggressive and smart.' (1)

1956   Brigitte began her graduate studies at IIT with Mies in Chicago on a Fulbright scholarship. Her first project was a square house with an open square staircase in the centre. Mies criticised the stair design and told her that 'if you can't do a good stair, hide it in a box.' She also began studying city planning with Ludwig Hilbersheimer and visual training with Walter Peterhans. She audited an undergraduate brick construction class and later took a wood construction class with Alfred Caldwell. She learned to draw construction details full-size, a habit she continued throughout her professional career.

1958   Brigitte continued her studies with Mies at IIT. She worked on the courtyard house design drawings and model, an IIT standard problem first taught by Mies at the Bauhaus. Building the model was challenging. Brigitte was the only female student, and the other male students ignored her and would not share information on where to purchase materials, so she wandered the city looking for sources. When Mies reviewed her model, where she had installed the building's columns at the last minute, he exclaimed that the columns looked like 'drunken soldiers' because they were not perfectly straight. A few weeks later Mies gave one of his typical reviews. He looked at the model silently for several minutes and then said that it was getting better and to keep working on it. She took a photography class with Aaron Siskind at IIT's Institute of Design. She became friends with John Vinci, David Sharpe, and Richard Nickel. She also started working part time at SOM. She married Walter Peterhans at City Hall during a lunchtime break from work. Her parents were sceptical of the age difference, but soon came to admire Peterhans. She began working full time at SOM in the interior design department and became friends with Jane Johnson, who later married architect Bruce Graham. Jane was originally from Austria, so there was a German language tie between them. She worked with Davis Allen on the Inland Steel corporate offices in the Inland Steel Building. This work included custom furniture design. She was then temporarily laid off from SOM, and travelled to California with Peterhans to visit his children from a prior wife. She visited Myron Goldsmith who was in the San Francisco office of SOM working on a United Airlines hangar. She then returned to Chicago SOM to work with Bruce Graham on the interiors of Upjohn corporate headquarters in Kalamazoo, Michigan.

1959 Mies was forced to retire from IIT. Brigitte travelled to Germany in the summer with Peterhans. She resumed studies at the University of Stuttgart while he looked for work at the Hamburg Art School. She finished her diploma at the University of Stuttgart and returned to Chicago alone in the fall.

1960 Walter Peterhans died while visiting Brigitte's parents in Stetten. Brigitte attended the funeral and then returned to Chicago to continue working on the Upjohn project. Jane Johnson married Bruce Graham and had to leave SOM. Brigitte asked Bruce if she could leave the interiors department and work in the architecture department. Her wish being granted, she worked on the Chicago Equitable building with Natalie de Blois and Pao-Chi Chang. She then worked on a small bank with David Haid. Having no children of her own, she volunteered to babysit for the children of David Haid, Bruce Graham, and Natalie de Blois.

Chapter—Life Chronology

1961 Brigitte completed her master's thesis at IIT with Daniel Brenner as advisor.

1963 Brigitte travelled solo with a Volkswagen Beetle through Mexico for two months, including visits with architects Luis Barragan and Felix Candela. She then returned to work in Germany at her father's request that she design buildings for his, and possibly other, Diakonies.

1964 Preferring not to work on 'family' projects, Brigitte began working in the Munich office of architect Peter von Seidlein, where fellow workers include the young Helmut Jahn.

1966 Brigitte returned to Stuttgart to work in the Stuttgart office of Heinle-Wischer and Partners on the competition for the 1972 Munich Olympics. Her brother Jörg was also working on the Olympic stadiums under structural engineer Fritz Leonhardt, with the architects Günter Behnisch and Frei Otto. Brigitte was offered a partnership at Heinle-Wischer but instead she left to design buildings for her father's Diakonie and a house for her parents.

1969 Brigitte attended a lecture in Stuttgart by SOM engineer Fazlur Khan. It inspired her and, frustrated with German architectural practice, she returned to Chicago SOM. She moved into an apartment in the Hancock Tower. Initially she worked on the Sears Tower Design, mostly on interior details (escalators, elevators, lighting, entrances, and signage) and exterior stairs and plaza fountains. She then began work as senior designer on Baxter Travenol corporate campus in Deerfield, Illinois. Work there included cooperation with Sasaki on the landscape design, and Institute of Design alumna Barbara Crane on a photographic art program for the campus.

1973 Brigitte was promoted to an associate at SOM.

1975 Brigitte began work on the Arab International Bank (AIB) project in Cairo, Egypt. In preparation, she travelled through Spain to see Moorish architecture and to Cairo and Luxor to see Egyptian architecture. She opened the SOM office in Cairo to do construction documents and oversee the construction of AIB. Work on the project included collaboration with the Spanish ceramic artist Artigas. The project was halted in mid-construction due to a lack of financing.

1979 Brigitte returned to Chicago SOM to work as senior designer on the new SOM offices at 33 West Monroe. The artist Chryssa was commissioned to design a light sculpture for the atrium. Chryssa and Brigitte became good friends as a result of this collaboration, and Brigitte designed Chryssa's loft renovation in Soho, New York. Brigitte was then promoted to associate partner and was given her own studio to lead. At this time, no woman had been made a general partner at SOM. She then bought and moved into a condominium in the Mies designed 910 North Lake Shore drive with furniture and other artworks originally owned by Peterhans and designed by Mies, Lily Reich, and others from the Bauhaus. Around this time Brigitte also befriended the eccentric Chicago street artist Lee Godie, who only sold her works to people she liked. Lee was homeless and slept on the street, but Brigitte often invited her to her apartment, even one time letting her spend the night there. The next morning, Lee served Brigitte tea in bed, claiming that the only other person so served was the Queen of England. Recalling her early years in the Diakonie, Brigitte herself said, 'All my friends were mentally retarded people. So, this is why I still now feel very close to such people. I have picked up quite a few mentally retarded or bipolar, crazy people here in the streets, and taken them to safety. Many of the street people are very good, just helpless. I have a very strong relationship to mentally troubled people.' (1) In her last will and testament, she left a substantial part of her estate to the Chicago Coalition for the Homeless.

1980 Brigitte began work on a competition for a high-rise office building in Minneapolis. She took the entire design team on a field trip to Minneapolis, including a stop in Winona, Minnesota to see a Louis Sullivan designed bank. She also began work on the Terraces at Perimeter Center office complex located in Atlanta, Georgia. At Perimeter Center she worked again with ceramic artist Artigas, and would later design the Artigas Foundation complex in Spain.

1988 Brigitte moved to the SOM London office to work on the Exchange House office building. During this time construction on AIB resumed, and she travelled to Cairo several times to oversee construction.

1991 Brigitte retired early from SOM, after Bruce Graham retired. She had worked only with Bruce Graham throughout her career at SOM. The other design partners did not have the patience to work with her as she had spoken her mind critically and did not suffer fools gladly, including even with clients. One example, 'I remember there was one meeting with Mr. [William] Graham (CEO of Baxter) where he said he wanted something significant. He was not crazy about what we previously showed him. He said, "Couldn't we put the executive building on top of the cafeteria?" And I said "Yes. And add it as a little tower and call it Baxter City." And he said, "Shut up!" Well, to say Baxter City, you know, was kind of not nice. I was kicked out of the meeting. I refused to go back in. Bruce and Bill Hartmann followed me. And I said, "I'm not going to work for this man again. Why can't I say something like this?" They said, "That's a little too much. You have to tone it down." But later on, when I was in meetings again [Willliam] Graham was very friendly to me, and I heard from Bruce years later that Mr. Graham said to him that he thought I was great.' (1) Fortunately, Bruce Graham was willing to work with and tolerate Brigitte and what he sometimes called her crazy ideas. Was this because he respected her design sense or because she was best friends with his wife, Jane Graham? Both, I imagine.

After retiring from SOM, Brigitte moved to a small house owned by her brother Jörg in Stuttgart, and began designs for a new multi-family residence on that site.

1996   Brigitte returned to Chicago. She worked as a design consultant with Sae Oh Architects and with David Fleener Architects. She designed renovations to houses in Berlin owned by her nephew Frieder Schlaich and for her niece Sibylle Schlaich as well as in Waiblingen for her nephew Florian Schlaich. She continued to travel extensively throughout Europe, China, Morocco, Iran, Greece, and Egypt. Several nieces, and nephews from Germany visited her in Chicago for long stays. Her nephew Mike Schlaich bought the Chicago condominium and the house in Stuttgart, allowing her to stay there as long as she lived.

2021   Brigitte passed away in Stuttgart Katharinen Hospital while visiting her brother Peter Schlaich. In her last weeks she was nursed by her nephew Florian Schlaich and his wife Anne. She is buried next to Walter Peterhans in the Schlaich family plot in Stetten. Her nephew Mike Schlaich will keep the apartment and the furniture in Chicago as she left it, for family members to stay in when visiting Chicago. A tea set designed by Bauhaus artist Marianne Brandt, a painting by German artist Lovis Corinth, and other art works from the apartment were donated by Brigitte to the Smart Museum of Art at the University of Chicago.

Brigitte Peterhans' childhood home, Kernen-Stetten, Germany _ Author

Brigitte Peterhans' apartment, 910 Lake Shore Drive, Chicago, Illinois: MR chairs, daybed, and Tugendhat chair by Mies van der Rohe; Parsons table by Mies as modified by Walter Peterhans; leather desk by Lili Reich. _ 900-910 Condo Association

ARCHITECTURAL EDUCATION AT IIT

Brigitte's studies at the Illinois Institute of Technology (IIT) were seminal in forming her design sensibilities and in establishing friends that would last her lifetime. In 1938, Mies van der Rohe accepted the position of director of the Armour Institute (later IIT) Department of Architecture. Prior to that, Mies had been director of the Bauhaus school in Germany, which had been closed by the Nazis in 1933. Joining him at IIT were two other Bauhaus teachers, Ludwig Hilbersheimer and Walter Peterhans. Prior to Mies' arrival, the school had followed Beaux-Arts classicism. Mies accepted the new position with the understanding that he would develop a totally new curriculum. The undergraduate program was designed to show the student 'what is possible in construction, what is necessary for use, and what is significant as art.'
The first year focused on architectural and life drawing. The second year introduced construction in brick and wood and the Visual Training (see below) series. The third year continued investigating structure in steel and concrete with additional work in Visual Training and the introduction of planning. The fourth year began the exploration of architecture as space and the integration of art, initiated with the Courtyard House Problem (see below.) The fifth year continued architectural investigations with larger scale structures and added the course in city and regional planning. Graduate students who transferred from other schools were required to take some undergraduate courses. Two that significantly influenced Brigitte were Visual Training and the Courtyard House (Space) Problem.

Visual Training
Based on earlier fundamental courses at the Bauhaus taught by Paul Klee, Wassily Kandinsky, and Johannes Itten, Visual Training at IIT was a course developed by Walter Peterhans which served to 'train the eye and sense of design and to foster aesthetic appreciation in the world of proportions, forms, colours, textures, and spaces.'(3) All of the exercises were produced on 20 inch × 30 inch white Strathmore board. The first set of exercises used straight and curved lines and planes of black paper to define spatial and rhythmic relationships. Further exercises used coloured and textured planes to define space and harmonious relationships, repetitive strokes in ink by brush and other tools to create visual texture,

and the chance dropping of watercolour on a wet board to create free form shapes. Peterhans was a student of philosophy at the University of Göttingen in the 1920s, where questions of epistemology, or the philosophy of science, became his philosophical heritage, and included such themes as 'the methodology of education, the nature of learning, the concept of objective taste, the concept of meta-aesthetics, and the definition of beauty.'(6) In contrast to the traditional method of teaching aesthetics through observation of historical prototypes, Peterhans argued 'we must presuppose aesthetic intuition, free creation by the constructive imagination, in order to pass from nature to the picture.'(7) Peterhans considered Visual Training as 'training of a distinct sort of intuition, leading to a heightened sensitivity to visual form. Once these sorts of abstract forms become visible, aesthetic judgment becomes better.'(6)

In addition to his studies in philosophy and mathematics, Peterhans was a noted photographer who taught the photography course at the Bauhaus. However, he abandoned the teaching of photography when developing the Visual Training class at IIT to focus not on technique but on the expression of proportion through form and material. 'The effect of the Visual Training course was a radical change in the whole mental attitude of the students. All fussiness and sloppiness disappeared from their work; they learned to discard any line that did not fulfil a purpose, and a real understanding of proportion emerged. Although specially gifted students sometimes produced plates that would have enriched the collection of a museum, the purpose of the course was never to produce works of art, but to train the eyes.'(Mies)

Courtyard House (Space) Problem
The courtyard house was a pedagogical problem first used by Mies at the Bauhaus. For fourth year students at IIT it was distilled down to a simple rectangular space enclosed by four brick bearing walls. A roof covering a portion of the site was placed atop the walls and further supported by two interior steel columns; full height glass walls separated the interior space from the outdoor courtyards. Programmatically, it could be a house or a museum, but the program was secondary to using the model to explore how interior walls of different heights, lengths, and colours could define the

interior space. After studying the model, plans for a specific program, and collages integrating paintings and sculptures, were prepared.

In addition to these two undergraduate courses, Brigitte also took the second year undergraduate wood construction semester taught by Alfred Caldwell where she learned to draw full-size details, a practice she followed throughout her career.

Mies van der Rohe, Walter Peterhans, and Ludwig Hilbersheimer at IIT _ Photographer Unknown

MASTER THESIS

Author's note: Included here is the entire text of Brigitte's Master Thesis as it reflects much of the philosophy of Mies and Hilbersheimer, while at the same time reflecting her unique study of, and experience of, European architecture, specifically the references to the use of light in Baroque architecture. It is also typical of the pedagogical method at IIT at that time. The text itself is both more interesting and more important than the actual building design.

Students' International House
Brigitte Eva Schlaich, Master Thesis, 1961
Advisor: Daniel Brenner

Preface
Tall buildings are characteristic of our time. They are free-standing buildings. Their structure clearly expresses their interior space organisation. In ordered groups of buildings inner and outer space become interrelated purposefully as well as artistically. Soundless, but well ordered, space, - concentrated, shaped, and interrelated by buildings, is characteristic for our time. This thesis title is 'Students' International House.' Equally well the title might have been 'A tall and a low building'. While 'International House' defines the program of the project by the indication of its purpose, 'A tall and a low building' defines the architectural problem as the study of the relations in a group of two differently sized, differently shaped, and free-standing buildings.

Chapter I – Introduction
Architecture and Space
Any enclosed space intentionally designed or provided by nature, offering protection from the elements, and satisfying the basic needs of a human being, may be called a shelter. Elaborated upon, made more permanent and comfortable and serving specific needs, material and spiritual ends, the shelter may become a building. But even a building well done may not yet be good architecture. For it is not enough for us that our material ends be served well. Above the demand for the solution of functional,

structural, economic, and social problems, is another and different factor:
The disinterested desire for beauty.

'Well building hath three conditions: Commodity, Firmness, and Delight. Architecture for consistency is a focus where three separate purposes have converged. They are blended in a single method: they are fulfilled in a single result; yet in their own nature they are distinguished from each other by a permanent disparity.' (Geoffrey Scott, *The Architecture of Humanism* (London: Constable & Co., 1914, 1947))
By itself the sound structure does not yet provide convenience; firmness and commodity do not grant yet delight. The structure must be so arranged as to obtain firmness, it must be so ordered as to provide expected services, it must take such a shape as to give delight. The structural shape is complex. The proportions of and within its façades are as important as its three-dimensional sculptural qualities. It extends horizontally as well as vertically. It forms a shell enclosing space as well as a volume reaching into space. It is to provide space usable for our needs that a structure is built, but it is a well-ordered space which instils delight and transforms a building into architecture. To shape space is the
architect's foremost problem.
'*Das Primaere alles architectonischen Gestaltens ist das Raumgefuehl ... Die Struckturformen, Gliederungen und Details sind nur eine Sichtbarmachung dieses Gefuehls in Material durch kuenstlerische Taetigkeit.*' (A. E. Brinkmann, *Platz und Monument*, (Berlin: Ernst Wasmuth Verlag, 1923))

Translation: 'The primary principle of architectural creation is the perception of and feeling for space ... structural form, articulation, order, and detail only become concrete as this feeling manifests itself through artistic activity.'

Historical Space Concepts
The spirit of an age pervades its social life, its religion, its scholarship, and its arts. Throughout the history of architecture 'Das Raumgefuehl' – the space concept – has changed and has forced its formal expression in the architectural 'styles'.

Architecture is not only the product of structure and materials, nor of diverse purposes and social conditions; it is, also, the result and manifestation of the changing spiritual life of successive periods – the product of a creativity nourished from, but rising above, the many energies that shape and condition an age.
It was not alone the invention of the arch and vault that made the quiet harmony of the clear sculptural body of a Greek temple develop into the magic, driving rhythm of a Byzantine basilica's interior space. It was not the space limitation within the military fortifications of the medieval city that made the verticality of a Gothic cathedral rise from narrow streets. Neither did their disappearance create the wide Baroque piazza within the city or place the princely palace and palace-like monastery into the vast parks outside the city, thus for the first-time juxtaposing architecture within nature. No innovations of structures or materials had any influence when, also in the Baroque, light was discovered as an architectural medium, when the interior and exterior began to unite in churches filled with light through clear glass windows, often concealed so as to make invisible the boundary between inside and outside.

New Space Concepts
The desire for buildings permeated with light existed before steel frame and reinforced concrete construction were at our disposal, allowing buildings to become glass-sheathed skeletons. Decentralisation was introduced before cities turned into slums, before traffic patterns paralysed our industrial and commercial centres. Industrialisation at first seemed to completely interrupt the gradual development towards open space and the free interplay with nature which architecture and city planning were engaged in until the first third of the last century, only to find itself by sheer necessity reintroducing it on an extended scale, sustained by a new technology 80 years later. However, with the changes towards a new pattern of urban civilisation forced upon us, these changes are made not only hesitatingly but are measures, for the most part, capable of offering only temporary relief.
In the end, the old city complex will have to be replaced by an entirely new organism. Its seeds exist, and a few projects demonstrate the possibility inherent in new and decisive ideas. They demonstrate what the new cities could be: healthy, well-func-

tioning, and spacious human settlements, set in and surrounded by a natural park. The park would grow into the private gardens of the single-family residences, surround the tall apartment buildings, and pass into a variety of squares. There would be a free and continuous interchange of closed and open spaces, an informal interrelation of structures of different kinds, varying in function, size and shape, enhancing certain centres of public importance by creating outstanding groups and spaces. The grouping of buildings thus became one of the essential architectural problems of today. It is in this relation that Frank Lloyd Wright's early prairie houses, considered by some to be the first buildings in which the original style of the twentieth century can be recognised, reveal their essential importance. While conceived without taking advantage of the newly developed structures and materials, steel skeleton and glass skin of the Chicago School's commercial buildings, their spatial quality exerted its influence upon European architecture; their freely spreading ground plans, the choice of the right site, the interweaving of exterior and interior by means of terraces and cantilevered roofs, by opening up one room into another, and by the tendency of the house to be as far as possible one room, one space melting into its surroundings.

Chapter II – Definition of the Problem

This thesis deals with the grouping of buildings as a partial and strictly architectural study, an aspect out of the complex problem of our time, the replanning of the old city.

The Architectural Problem – A Tall and a Low Building

The tall building (skyscraper) was developed from social, economical, and technical conditions. The original motive to build vertically is more and more giving way to the new desire for open space and the interest in the plastic quality of the juxtaposition of the free-standing tall and / or lower buildings. As has been stated in the Introduction, the combination of one tall and one low building was chosen as the architectural problem of this thesis.

The project can be expected to be involved with the following problems:
Formally: the composition of a vertical and a horizontal structural form and their spatial relationship. Functionally: one large integrated space of easy accessibility. Numerous spaces of various sizes, but of similar use with limited relationship to each other, but with equal relationship to the large space (e.g. typical for a hotel, hospital, many office buildings, etc.) Structurally: structures for both buildings, functionally and economically as well as aesthetically satisfying.

The Specific Problem – Students' International House
Is the combination of a tall and a low building necessarily the solution for a students' international house? To answer this question, an explanation should be given first of what is understood by international house: a hotel-like building where students lodge, usually connected with recreational facilities where students gather to spend their leisure time. Preferably these buildings should be located close to the centre of the university, together with the administration, main auditorium, library, museums, etc. For functional reasons the international house is best represented by several buildings, separating the living quarters from the recreational area.
In the present studies, an international house has been planned for the campus of the University of Chicago. A program for the basic requirements of the project has been developed after consideration of existing buildings of similar character. For the lodging quarters the planning should offer rooms wide-ranging in size, but equal in quality, and also allow variation in living arrangements. Preference should be given to the single study bedroom, including a private bathroom. All rooms should have generous storage space. Approximately 70 per cent should be single rooms, including a bathroom, their sizes ranging from approximately 250 to 500 square feet, including the bathroom and storage. The largest type could be rented to two students. Approximately 20 per cent should be efficiency apartments, including a kitchenette, to be rented to married students and teachers. The rest should be one-to-three bedroom apartments. Sufficient entrance and service facilities have to be provided, including mail room, switchboard, housing office, technical installation, workshop, storage, etc.

For maximum variation in the use of the recreational facilities, the space provided should be as flexible as possible, serving the three different functions:

1. Space which will serve as a social meeting place, auditorium for informal lectures, plays or concerts, a small library offering actual literature, newspapers, magazines, lounge area for discussions, TV, radio, play, including some separate meeting places for clubs, student conferences, etc. and some offices.
2. A cafeteria with a self-service counter.
3. Subsidiary elements, such as coat-rooms and restrooms, kitchen service, technical installation, workshop, and storage.

For both programs, besides sufficient outdoor area and well-located entrances for the students, a service entrance should be provided, but must not interfere with the pedestrian circulation. Proper provision for parking is necessary, but should be located away from the building so as not to dominate the site. The buildings should be well-related to the environment, and the site should be landscaped to give the whole area a pleasant appearance.

Chapter III – Development of the Project

As has been stated before, it was decided to restrict the project of this study to a partial problem: the planning of student accommodations for the existing campus of the University of Chicago. A complete redevelopment of the whole campus would be another and most actual problem, but reached far beyond the frame of an architectural thesis.
A specific site on the campus of the University of Chicago was chosen: the area, enclosed by 57th and 59th Streets, Woodlawn and Kenwood Avenues, seemed to be the most suitable; facing the park-like Midway towards the south, being well located in relation to the academic center towards the west and north-west and the residential quarters of the university towards the east and north-east.

Site Function and Plan

The development of the site involves three major elements: building, parking, and services. It was considered to be best to reserve the site along the Midway for the buildings and separate the parking north along 59th Street. 58th Street and Kimbark Avenue, dividing the area into four equal rectangles, were to be closed for traffic, both being dead end streets already. 58th Street has been closed for through traffic between Kenwood and University Avenues, thus being safe for pedestrian circulation between the university center and international house. Kimbark Avenue has been completely taken out between Midway and 58th Street. The two blocks along 59th Street, between Woodlawn and Kenwood Avenues, are now occupied by several three to four-storey buildings, housing various residential student facilities. They have been taken out.

The decision to combine a tall and a low building was not immediately arrived at. It involved many considerations. Extensive studies revealed that tall buildings for the living quarters are dictated by the number and kind of facilities to be provided on the given site. A tall building for the housing facilities and a low building for the recreational activities were accepted as being the best solution, functionally as well as architecturally. The planning began with the quantitative determination of the program: the number of students to be housed, and depending on that, the space to be provided as recreational area. In the existing buildings on the site, approximately 500 students live in dormitories and approximately 150 in residences. This number, approximately 650 people, was considered as the minimum requirement for the new international house. Recreational facilities should be adequate and include a cafeteria with a capacity for 550 meals to be served in two sittings. Buildings for the residential quarters were systematically studied, investigating the various possibilities: walk-up buildings, multi-storey buildings, buildings with rooms only south oriented, etc. Walk-up buildings were ruled out because they would occupy the whole site too densely; groupings of two, three, or four buildings did not lead to any valuable site plan, especially not in relation to the recreational facilities and the environment; exclusive south orientation of all buildings and rooms did not result in any architectural solution.

In studies on a preliminary model, a 20-storey building for the housing program, 60 feet wide by 240 feet long, combined with a one-storey building for the recreational program, 180 feet wide by 240 feet long, was finally accepted. They are placed at right angles to each other, opening towards the campus center. This serves functional requirements in the least complicated way, and at the same time, achieves architectural contrast and a feeling of spaciousness. The tall building is east-west oriented along Kenwood Avenue. All four exposures are utilised by the living units. Their view is equally good: they can all see the park; in addition, the east side overlooks the lake, the west side the plaza and the campus. Since the site slopes slightly towards the Midway, it was possible to carry on the level of the north end and raise a terrace-like platform along the Midway, approximately five feet above level at its highest point. The long south side of the recreational building has a good view into the Midway from this terrace.

Single family residences are now located on the site being reserved for car parking. Their architectural quality and physical condition does not make it worthwhile to save them, except a few along the former 58th Street – Frank Lloyd Wright's Robie House among them – where they and their gardens could beneficially screen off the mass of parked cars. The parking lot would be entered by car from 57th Street. Pedestrian entries would lead directly to the buildings. Temporary parking space for a few cars could be arranged at the east side of the tall building.

The problem of service is best handled when completely separated from indoor and outdoor living quarters and pedestrian circulation. This is done by making use of a service ramp and a tunnel leading into and out of an extended basement connecting and serving the two buildings underground.

The Structural System and Architectural Concept

In selecting the structural system for two buildings, which are different from each other in shape and different in function within themselves, but also related to each other by certain functions and therefore related by location, one problem has to be solved first: shall the structures basically be the same for both buildings, adapted to their different shapes, or shall they be different in principle? Both approaches were studied: the structures of two differently shaped and differently functioning buildings may or may not be the same. The best possible solution has to be studied and developed for both of them individually. A final conclusion may arrive at either solution.

As has been mentioned before, the structure for the tall building, housing the rooms and apartments, should permit greatest flexibility within the layout of the floors. This determines the structure to be a skeleton. One of the major problems in developing a skeleton is the placement of the columns. To find the most suitable skeleton, four systems were studied and compared:

1. A clear-span structure, with columns only at the outside of the building, was found to make sense only where the program would take advantage of the wide, completely uninterrupted spaces, e.g. for an office building.
2. The traditional interior column structure on a square bay size of approximately 20 feet and a module of approximately five feet, has been approved in many existing solutions for apartment buildings. However, there is a certain inflexibility: dividing the space into rooms along the exterior exposure, one is limited to either a four-module room width (approximately 20 feet) or half of it. In other words, the columns along the outside restrict the room sizes to two variations only, since it would be impossible to have a room with one window on one and one or two windows on the other side of a column; the dimensions of the column would destroy the scale of the room. This problem occurs whether windows are placed between the columns or on their outside as a skin.
3. It could only be avoided by having no columns in the window plane. One way to achieve this would be to recess the windows enclosing the interior space approximately three feet behind the face of the structural grid, which is exposed all around and which creates a shallow balcony arcade.
4. To recess the columns, as far as the depth of an average room, would be another possibility. Then the columns could be placed without further difficulties within the continuous, solid core of bathrooms, kitchens, closet space, and storage rooms, typical for any residential building. This means an

approximately 15-foot cantilever on all four sides of the building. Every floor would extend 15 feet over its column support, the columns being placed with a span of 30 feet. In other words, a relation of 1:2:1 cantilever, in the short direction; the placement of the columns in the long direction to be determined through further studies of the structure.

A special structure had to be found to solve this problem. The conventional one-way system does not apply well: whether in steel or concrete, the increased height of the main beams would interfere with the layout. A two-way system in steel, based on a square bay, results in a two-way truss. This method, developed for extremely wide spans in both directions, for big halls, auditoriums, etc., would not make sense for the comparatively small spans of a multi-storey building, and would also be too complicated and, therefore, too expensive in high-rise construction. The concrete mushroom structure is also based on the square bay, two-way system. Originally developed for heavy load bearing, industrial buildings or warehouses and longer spans, the self-supporting, reinforced slabs without any beams, uniformly bearing throughout their length and width, can be cantilevered out on both sides to carry supplementary loads. They are therefore ideal in combination with non-supporting walls, such as glass curtain walls. However, the mushroom head, necessarily used as a structural intermediate element, makes the employment of this system for our building impossible; the mushroom head cannot be accepted for the small-scale pattern of an apartment layout.

The waffle slab system solves the problem. Based on the structural principles of the mushroom system, it is essentially a flat slab of a thickness increased from approximately seven to 12 inches, with voids inserted to reduce the dead load without lessening the rigidity. Approximately 30-foot spans are considered to be the most economical; cantilevers in both directions are of advantage. Where the column meets the ceiling, the slab is solid, thus providing the intermediate zone to take the shear moments within the dimension of the slab. The system has been shown to be very economical and is commercialised by several companies (Portland Cement, Steeldome, Container Corporation of America, Liftslab Corporation). A structural estimate proved that the method could be well-applied to the 21-storey project. On a square bay of approximately 30 feet, the slabs would be 12.5 inches thick; the columns of the three top floors would be 10 by 10 inches, increasing towards the bottom floors in proportion with the loads, every three floors, by four inches in width and two inches in depth, which would make them 36 by 24 inches on the first floor. To obtain the wind bracing, an additional reinforced concrete frame would have to connect the columns, increasing from 12.5 inches on the 14th floor to 30 inches on the first floor.

At this point the functional requirements must be considered to determine the most advantageous bay size and module. The layouts of the various room units were developed and a module of five feet and four inches was found to be most desirable. The two-module room, as the smallest unit, should be at least 10 feet and six inches wide. Other rooms would be 16 feet wide. With the exception of the narrow rooms, which have to be deeper, location and dimension of the column determine the depth of the rooms, 14 feet, and the width of the bathrooms, six feet and seven inches. The bathrooms are best arranged in pairs. The closet and storage units readily interchange with the bathrooms, thus taking none of the valuable living space. Single rooms seem to be best located along the long sides of the building, the bigger apartments at its ends. Since the structure requires vertical opening in the slabs to be as close to the center of the bay as possible, elevator shafts and stairwells were placed as free-standing elements in the central corridor. Functionally, this arrangement proves to be also most suitable. Many entrances to a great number of small units would have overcrowded a single-branched hallway. Additional service facilities, such as janitor room, incinerator, storage space, and freight elevator, were combined with the stairwells. The complete layout is so organised as to permit the insertion of open lounge areas at either end, or at the center of, the corridor.

The five-foot-and-four-inch module determines the size of the coffers; voids are 30 inches square at two-foot-and-10-inch centres, meeting the ideal standards of the waffle system. Exact bay dimensions are 32 square feet, and cantilevers 16 feet. After the structural system had been decided on, in accordance with the functional requirements, the treatment of the curtain walls had to be studied. A continuous skin, sheathing the whole structure, seems to be the best: it not only protects the whole building simply and efficiently, it also assembles the mass of piled-up floors into one sculptural volume of unbroken verticality. A curtain wall is supported by mullions. To shape the mullion is the essential problem, defining the character of the whole building. For structural reasons, a mullion spanning a height of approximately nine feet can be made very slim. However, a glass skin, enveloping a building 256 feet wide, 64 feet deep, and 220 feet high, does request more in order not to look like a sleek cellophane-wrapped box. For this reason, the I-beam shaped mullions have been introduced and successfully used for many recent buildings (860 and 900 Lake Shore Drive, Commonwealth Apartments, Seagram Building), whether done in steel, aluminium, bronze, etc.

Functional requirements of flexibility and spatial differentiation were decisive in selecting the structure for the low recreational building. A column system of evenly distributed interior columns on a square bay of approximately 30 feet was chosen rather than a free-span structure without interior columns. A free-span system makes good sense only when being used as a large undivided space, e.g. as a concert hall. An interior column system allows flexible subdivision of the space for various uses by the arrangement of free-standing non-supporting walls between columns without destroying the oneness of the space. Considerations of unity with regard to structure and appearance led to the adoption and adaptation to the low building of the structural system developed for the tall building. The same concrete waffle-grid slab that shapes the vertical structure, cantilevered from a two-by-eight series of tapering columns on 22 floors spreads as one flat slab of large area over a six-by-12 sequence of columns. The same bay, 32 feet square, and the same 16-foot cantilever that fits the functional requirements of successive apartment floors shelters the open plan development of the recreational area.

Yet, in spite of the sameness of the basic structure, the two buildings are of entirely different formal expression. One is tall and slender, rising vertically, tower-like; the other low, reaching out horizontally. One is a determined integration into verticality of numerous cells on successive horizontal planes; the other is generously expansive, holding within a few articulate elements, ordering the free-flow of a vast and open space.

To heighten the difference, the glass line of the low structure has been recessed behind the first row of columns. Similarly, the waffle grid is left uncovered indoors as well as outdoors. An interior garden court, 64 feet square, provides additional lighting and informality, and breaks up the monotony of the rooftop viewed from the apartments of the tall structure.

Chapter IV – Description of the Final Project
The project of a student international house for the University of Chicago consists of two buildings, a multi-storey building for the housing facilities, and a one-storey building for the recreational quarters. Both buildings are free-standing on a terrace-like, landscaped plaza, as a well-balanced and well-proportioned architectural group. They are easily accessible from all sides, their main entrances open to the plaza, which is again opened towards the close-by academic center of the campus. Automobile, pedestrian, and service circulations have been integrated into a functional, efficient pattern, which does not spoil the site nor disturb any living quarters, indoors or outdoors.

The Structure
Separate structural studies for the two buildings resulted in the same system for both: a reinforced concrete skeleton, on a square bay, cantilevering in all four directions. The major element is a two-way waffle grid, supported by a square column. A bay, 32 feet square, was found most efficient for both buildings; the cantilever is 16 feet. The module of the waffle grid is two feet and eight inches for the ground floor. A curtain wall is hung from the roof of the tall building to the second-floor level, independent of the skeleton. It consists of clear, thermopane glass supported by aluminium I-shaped mullions. Clear glass walls recessed behind the columns are enclosing the entrance hall on the first storey of the tall building. As an alternative, a curtain wall extending over all 21 storeys, with channel shaped mullions and grey tinted glass, has been developed. Free-standing walls, differing in material, size, and proportion, form the exterior and interior of the main floor of the low structure. The materials are glass, stone, and wood. The interior court is enclosed by clear glass

walls. The floor is laid with light marble; the same surfacing is used all around the buildings and also for the flooring in the entrance of the tall building.

The Plan
The tall building provides rooms for approximately 700 students on 20 high-rise floors of 64 feet by 256 feet. They are accessible from the ground floor entrance hall by four elevators. The typical floor layout shows room and apartment units all around the central corridor, in which elevator shaft and stairwells are free-standing. Room units for single students are two, three and four modules wide and of various depth. They all have their own bathrooms and built-in closets and storage space. They are proportioned and arranged as to allow efficient and also variable furnishing. The four-module room could also be occupied by two students. A special unit, two small rooms with one entrance and one bathroom, offers a most economical arrangement for two students, and also separation of bedroom and study for each person. Efficiency apartments and one-, two-, and three-bedroom apartments are provided for married students and teachers. The layout is such as to permit the central corridor to open up to the exterior in several ways, thus providing lounge area within the floors. The ground floor serves as a spacious, all-glass entrance hall. The north lobby, being the main entrance, opens towards both sides, plaza and street; it is connected with mail and storage rooms. Mezzanines provide the required space for the housing office, switchboard, etc. They are accessible through the enclosed stairwells. The basement contains the technical installations, laundry, workshop, and storage. It is connected with the basement of the recreational building by an extension functioning as an underground service court.
The low building for the recreational facilities can be described as part of the terrace on which both buildings are placed. On ground level a large inner and outer space is created, defined by free-standing, non-supporting walls and by groups of trees and the different planes of a pool, lawn, and pavement. This whole area serves as an indoor and outdoor plaza where students meet in their free time.
The lobby is entered from the plaza. Library, offices, and meeting rooms surround the square patio. The cafeteria and outdoor dining terrace face Midway and south.

Towards the west, large lounge spaces combine with a sheltered outdoor area and a large garden court. Two wide stairs connect the first-floor entrance directly with the auditorium and its lobby in the basement. Additional recreational facilities and the required coat-rooms, restrooms, kitchen, and services are also located in the basement.

Chapter V – Summary

1. The conception of a tall building combined with a low building seems to be a sensible solution for the problem of a student's international house. It will provide spaciousness as well as privacy and a modest amount of comfort, appropriate to a university campus.
2. A skeleton enclosed by a glass and aluminium curtain wall is a reasonable solution for a 12-storey-high building housing 700 students. For the low building, sheltering and the manifold recreational facilities, the same structure has been used, providing a very adequate system for both types of buildings.
3. The chosen column system of 32 feet square and a 16-foot cantilever allows all the flexibility required by the project.

Figure 12. View from North west

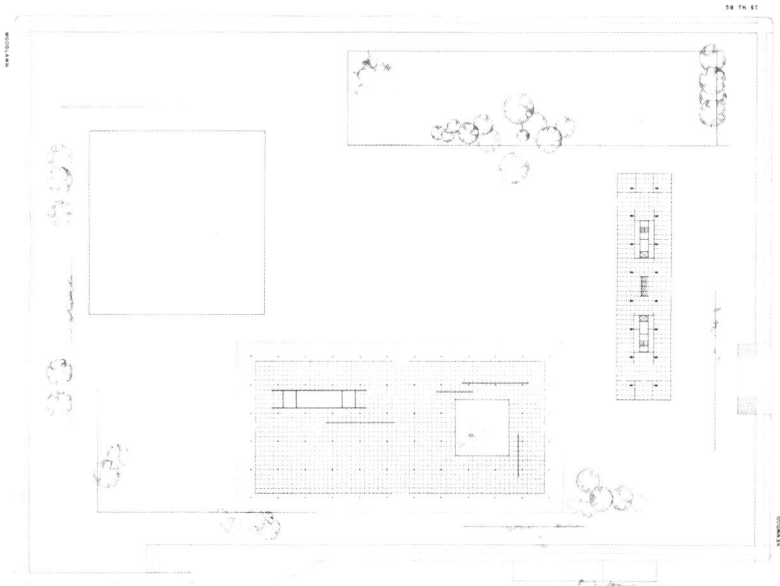

Figure 1. Site and Ground Floor Plan

Master's Thesis Model and Site Plan

58 — 59

WORK AT SKIDMORE, OWINGS & MERRILL

Inland Steel Building, Corporate Headquarters
Chicago, Illinois 1958

This 19-storey corporate office building for the Inland Steel Corporation has a unique plan with all of the core services (elevators, stairs, toilet rooms) in a separate tower allowing for an unobstructed and column-free open office space. An acoustical metal pan ceiling was designed to accept movable, modular, steel, and glass partitions. Despite the debate over whether the senior designer was Bruce Graham or Walter Netsch, Brigitte worked with Jane Johnson (later Jane Graham) and Davis Allen on the interiors for the Inland Steel executive office suites, including many custom designed pieces of furniture for the office of the President's wife, Mary Block.

Inland Steel Corporation, Chicago, Illinois _ Hedrich Blessing

Inland Steel Corporation, Chicago, Illinois _ Hedrich Blessing

Inland Steel Corporation, Chicago, Illinois _ Hedrich Blessing

The Upjohn Company, Corporate Headquarters
Kalamazoo, Michigan 1961

This 286,000-square-foot office building was Bruce Graham's first of many corporate headquarters in a semi-urban setting. As with the future Baxter Travenol headquarters, Bruce insisted that buildings in a rural setting be white while buildings in an urban setting be black. The Upjohn building is a one-storey building with a space frame roof which is expressed in white aluminium cladding. Seven interior courtyard gardens with trees, pools, stones, and sculptures bring natural daylight to the interior. Like the Inland Steel building, the offices were divided by moveable steel and glass partitions. The custom ceiling panels reflect the space frame roof modules. As in the Inland Steel executive offices, Brigitte worked with Jane Johnson on the interiors, which included custom designed furniture. Sasaki Walker were the landscape architects, a collaboration that would continue on future projects. The building was demolished in 2007.

The Upjohn Company, Corporate Headquarters, Michigan _ Hedrich Blessing

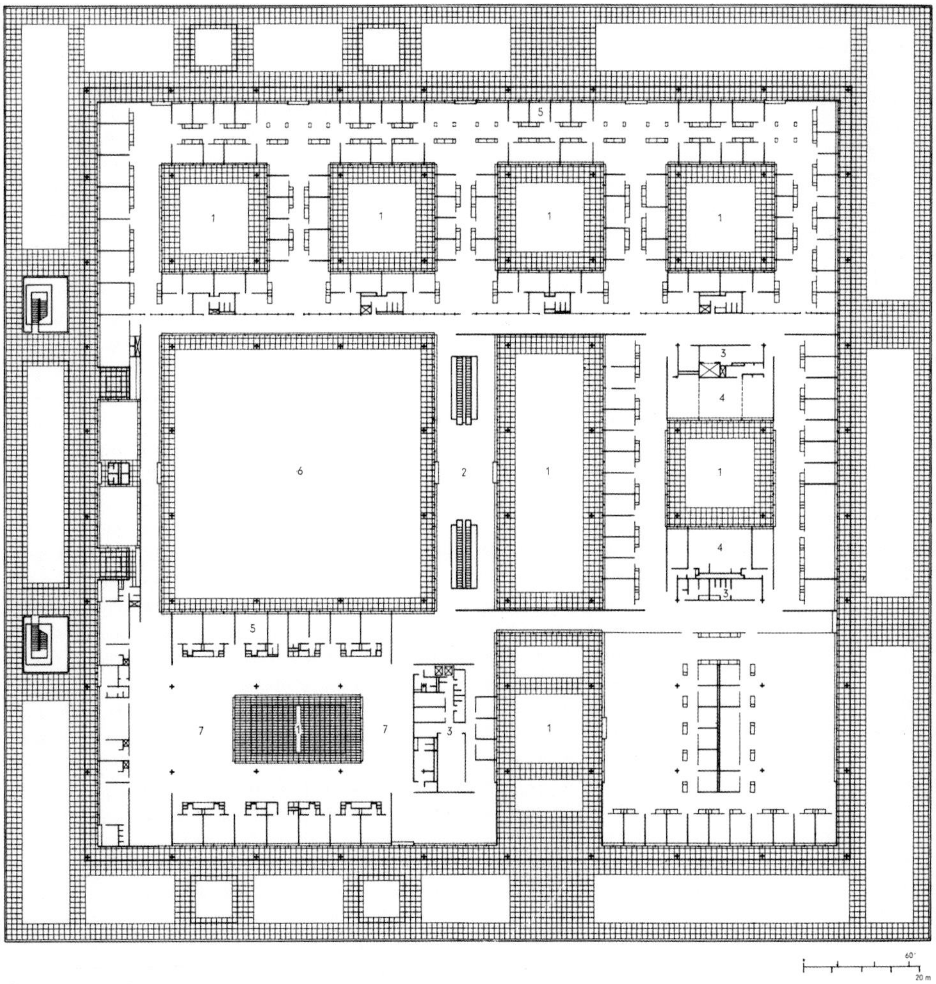

Plan, upper level / Grundriß Obergeschoß.
1 Inner courts / Innenhöfe
2 Escalators / Rolltreppen
3 Service cores / Servicekerne
4 Conference rooms / Konferenzräume
5 Individual offices / Einzelbüros
6 Large inner court / Großer Innenhof
7 Lounge / Aufenthaltsraum

Section / Schnitt.
1 Upper floor with entrance from upper level / Obergeschoß mit Eingang von der oberen Ebene
2 Ground floor with main entrance from lower level / Erdgeschoß mit Haupteingang von der unteren Ebene
3 Basement floor / Untergeschoß

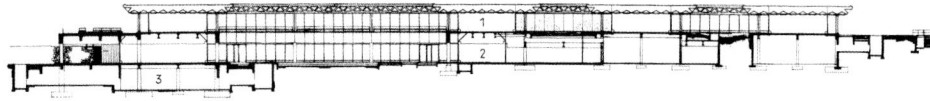

Upjohn Corporate Headquarters, Kalamazoo, Michigan _ ESTO

Chapter—Work at SOM

Upjohn Corporate Headquarters, Kalamazoo, Michigan _ ESTO

Equitable Building
Chicago, Illinois 1965

This 35-storey high-rise on Chicago's Magnificent Mile, adjacent to the Chicago River and the Tribune Tower was Brigitte's first work in the architecture department at SOM. In what may have been a first for the profession, she worked with two other women architects, Natalie de Blois, and Pao-Chi Chang. Brigitte's involvement on the project included work on the façade and the spiral stair leading from the plaza to a river sidewalk. In 2017, the stair was demolished, and the plaza reconfigured to accommodate a new Apple Store.

Equitable Building, Chicago, Illinois _ Hedrich Blessing

74 _ 75   Chapter—Work at SOM

Equitable Building, Chicago, Illinois _ Hedrich Blessing

Sears Tower
Chicago, Illinois 1973

Sears Tower is one of the most widely known SOM buildings and was the world's tallest building for many years. A building of this size and complexity required an equally large and complex team of architects and engineers. Brigitte was assigned the task of designing those elements that interact most with the occupants and visitors, including the plaza, entry, graphics, elevator cabs, and toilet rooms.

Sears Tower Plaza _ ESTO

Baxter Travenol Laboratories Inc., Corporate Headquarters
Deerfield, Illinois 1973–1985

The Baxter International Headquarters is a corporate campus in suburban Lake County, Illinois, completed in 1975, with a 1985 addition. The campus includes the Central Facilities Building, five office pavilions, an executive pavilion, and three parking garages. The parking garages are centrally located and surrounded by the office pavilions, thereby minimising the views of parking from the offices, and maximising the views of the landscape. These parking garages have a stepped design facing the office pavilions. Each of these steps contains a large concrete planter box, designed to hide the automobiles within. The twin masts of the Central Facilities Building's cable-stayed, suspended roof not only provide a focus for the site, but also create a local identity, visible from the nearby expressway. This was the first known use of a cable-stayed roof and was a result of the graduate thesis work being undertaken by Myron Goldsmith and Fazlur Khan at IIT. Significantly, other structural concepts developed at IIT were later used by SOM for exposed x-bracing at the John Hancock Tower in Chicago and the structural tube concept used for the Brunswick Building and the Sears (now Willis) Tower, all in Chicago. The Central Facility Building's large free-span interior houses an auditorium, training center and a 24-foot-high cafeteria. Large expanses of uninterrupted glass span each elevation of the building. The five office pavilions are four and five storeys in height with a clear-span structural system allowing for ultimate flexibility in original, as well as future, office layouts. Although served by a central mechanical plant, the individual pavilions are otherwise self-sufficient in terms of toilet rooms and other services. All of the buildings are clad with white painted steel.

The campus is surrounded by a landscape plan designed by Sasaki, Dawson, DeMay Associates that includes native plantings and a chain of eight man-made lakes that provide drainage, storm water retention, and flood control, features that were new for corporate campus design but are now standard. By 2022, Baxter had sold off many of its subsidiaries and the staff at the Deerfield headquarters was substantially reduced to less than 200 workers. In 2023, a developer proposed to buy the site, demolish the buildings, and erect a massive distribution center. Fortunately, the residential neighbours nearby made a big enough protest for the developer to abandon its plans.

Baxter Travenol Headquarters _ Grubman

Baxter Travenol Office Building, Deerfield, Illinois _ ESTO

Baxter Travenol Office Building, Deerfield, Illinois _ ESTO

Baxter Travenol Office Building, Deerfield, Illinois _ ESTO

Arab International Bank
Cairo, Egypt 1975

The purpose of this Bank is to carry out all the banking, financial and commercial activities related to the projects of economic development and foreign trade, especially for the interest of the member states and other Arab countries. The 1.5-million-square-foot project includes two 30-storey apartment towers, a 20-storey office tower for the Bank, a 600-room hotel, and a six-storey World Trade and Retail Center connecting the towers. The private development portions of the project were the financial engine for the bank portion.

Arab International Bank, Cairo, Egypt _ SOM

Chapter—Work at SOM

Arab International Bank, Cairo, Egypt _ Author

Chapter—Work at SOM

Arab International Bank, Cairo, Egypt _ Author

Skidmore, Owings & Merrill Offices

Chicago, Illinois 1980

33 West Monroe is a 29-storey office building designed by SOM for the developer Draper & Kramer. Designed during the energy crisis of the mid 1970s, it features a large floor plate with multiple interior atriums. As part of the agreement between the owner and the architect, SOM committed to relocating its offices there. At that time, SOM was at its peak, with 1,200 employees in Chicago. The area leased by SOM was 120,000 square feet: half of the second floor, all of floors three, four, and five, and half of the seventh floor. The fourth floor held offices for the general partners, many with custom designed furniture pieces. Custom millwork elements throughout the space included vending machine enclosures, coat closets, a full-scale kitchen, and a library. An open architectural steel stair was designed to connect the third, fourth, and fifth floors. The architectural and engineering studio work areas included custom-designed drafting stations and breakout areas with low tables called Kindergarten Tables where teams could informally meet to discuss their projects. The Kindergarten Tables were so popular they were carried over to future SOM offices in other buildings.

SOM Offices with Chryssa Sculpture, Chicago, Illinois _ Hedrich Blessing

The Terraces at Perimeter Center

Atlanta, Georgia 1986

Perimeter Center is an edge city located north of Atlanta, developed on what was 500 acres of farmland by the group Taylor & Mathis. While there are approximately 40,000 residents, the majority of the development is commercial office, hotel, and shopping malls. Taylor & Mathis commissioned SOM to design an office complex on a particularly scenic site there of heavily forested rolling hills. The development was built in two phases. Each phase consists of a pair of ten-storey office buildings connected by a full height atrium, and with a parking structure nestled into the landscape. The atrium concept was a further development of an idea originally used in the Chicago 33 West Monroe building, an idea to provide perimeter offices adjacent to the atriums with natural light and views while minimising open air heat gain. Expanding on this energy saving concept, Brigitte proposed setting the exterior glass back from the concrete structural frame and adding sunshades. This allowed the use of clear vision glass that was protected from direct solar exposure while maximising views of the surrounding nature, as opposed to the use of tinted and mirrored glass commonly used as an energy saving solution at that time. The exposed structural frame is evocative of a giant Sol Lewitt sculpture, which erodes as the upper storeys are set back to create the eponymous 'terraces'. The first floor of each atrium is paved with ceramic tiles in a colourful tapestry form by the Barcelona artist Joan Lorens Artigas. Warm wood framing is used for the interior atrium window frames, bridge guardrails, and the exposed wood and glass elevators. This use of wood is carried outside via the entry canopies and the cable suspended pedestrian bridges leading to the parking structures. Unlike many other clients, Mr. Taylor and Mr. Mathis were true southern gentlemen who loved and treated Brigitte with respect, like a southern belle.

The Terraces at Perimeter Center, Atlanta, Georgia _ Timothy Hursley

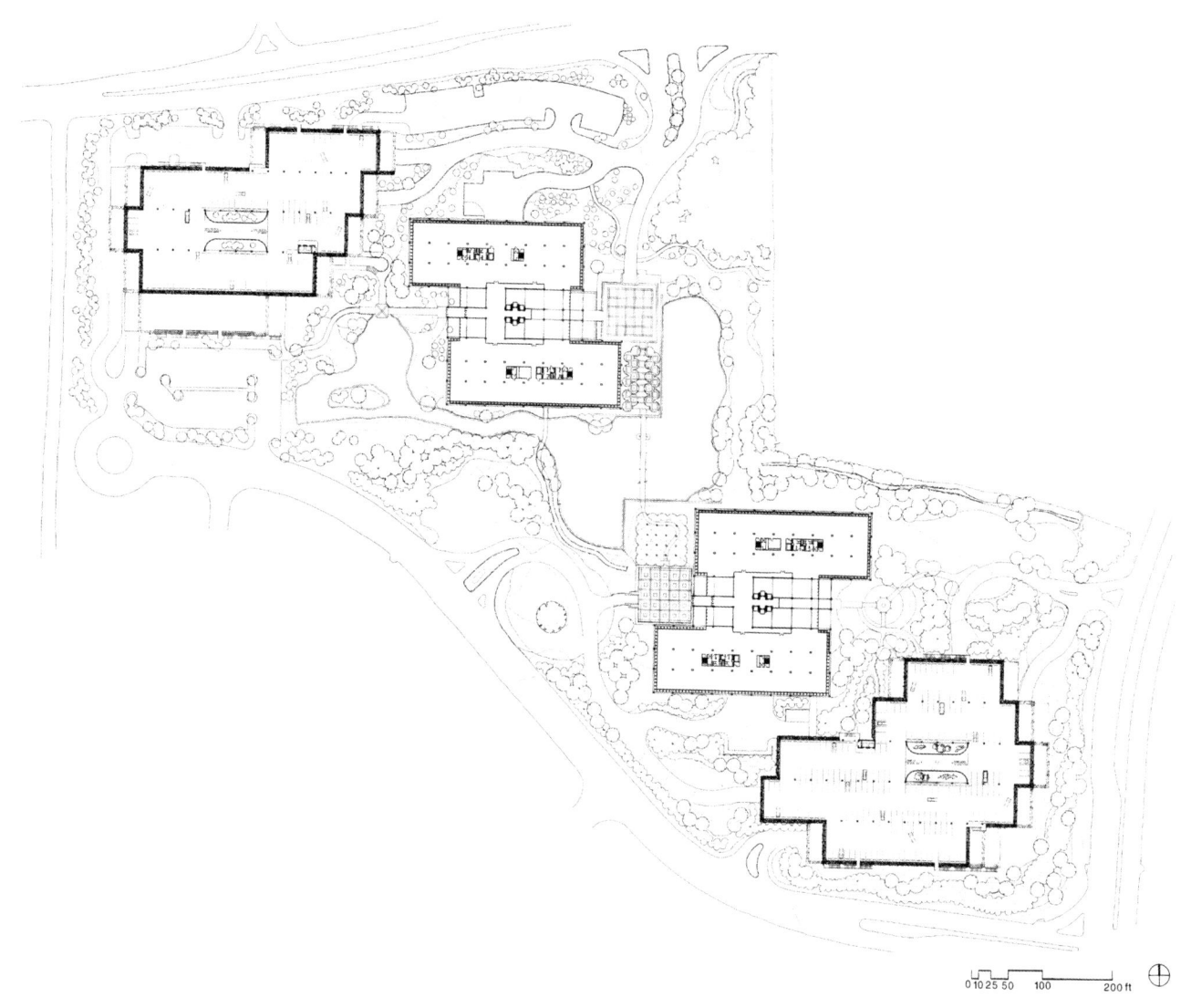

The Terraces at Perimeter Center, Site Plan, Atlanta, Georgia _ SOM

The Terraces at Perimeter Center, Atlanta, Georgia _ Timothy Hursley

The Terraces at Perimeter Center, Atlanta, Georgia _ Timothy Hursley

The Terraces at Perimeter Center, Atlanta, Georgia _ Timothy Hursley

Josep Llorens Artigas Foundation Studio
Gallifa, Barcelona, Spain 1989

In 1989, the Josep Lorens Artigas Foundation was created in memory of the famous ceramicist by his sculptor son, Joan Gardy Artigas. In addition to their own ceramic work, they have collaborated with and helped to realise the works of such artists as Braque, Picasso, Chagall, Miro, and Giacometti. The Foundation buildings include housing and studios for visiting professional artists from around the world.
The Foundation also organises exhibitions, concerts, conferences, and meetings between art critics, professors, and other personalities of art and culture. The first exposure of Artigas to SOM was when he was commissioned to produce the ceramic tiles on a Miro sculpture in Chicago that was structurally engineered by SOM. During his visits to Chicago, Bruce Graham asked Brigitte to look after him and consequently they became friends. Brigitte later worked on two projects that included ceramic tiles created by Artigas: the Terraces at Perimeter Center and the Arab National Bank in Cairo. The Foundation is located in a mountainous, forested area near Barcelona, and the various buildings reflect the traditional architecture of the area, using stucco, brick, and sloped red tile roofs, illustrating Brigitte's ability to design in a language other than strictly Miesian, and appropriate to its setting.

Artigas Foundation Studios, Barcelona, Spain _ Sibylle Schlaich

Chapter—Work at SOM

Artigas Foundation Studios, Barcelona, Spain _ Sibylle Schlaich

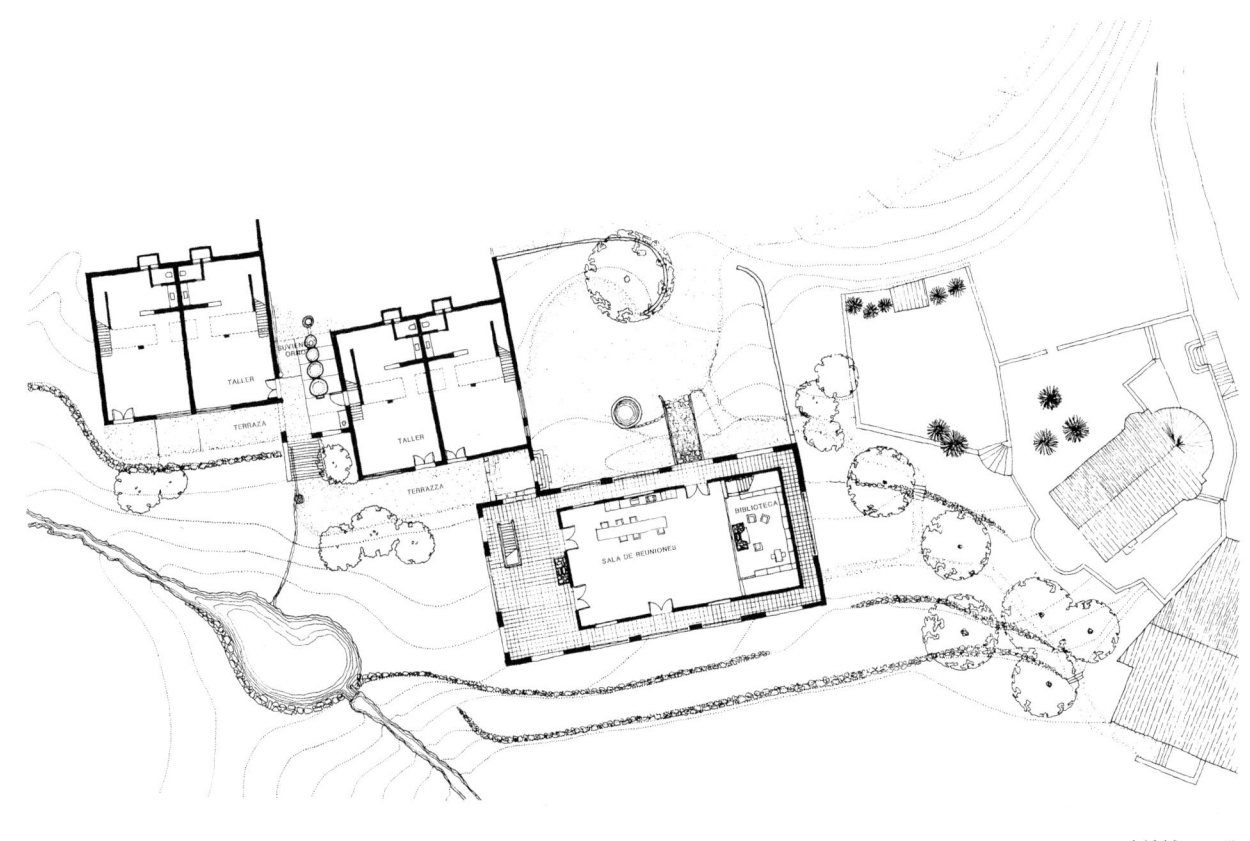

MAIN FLOOR PLAN

TALLERS J. LLORENS ARTIGAS

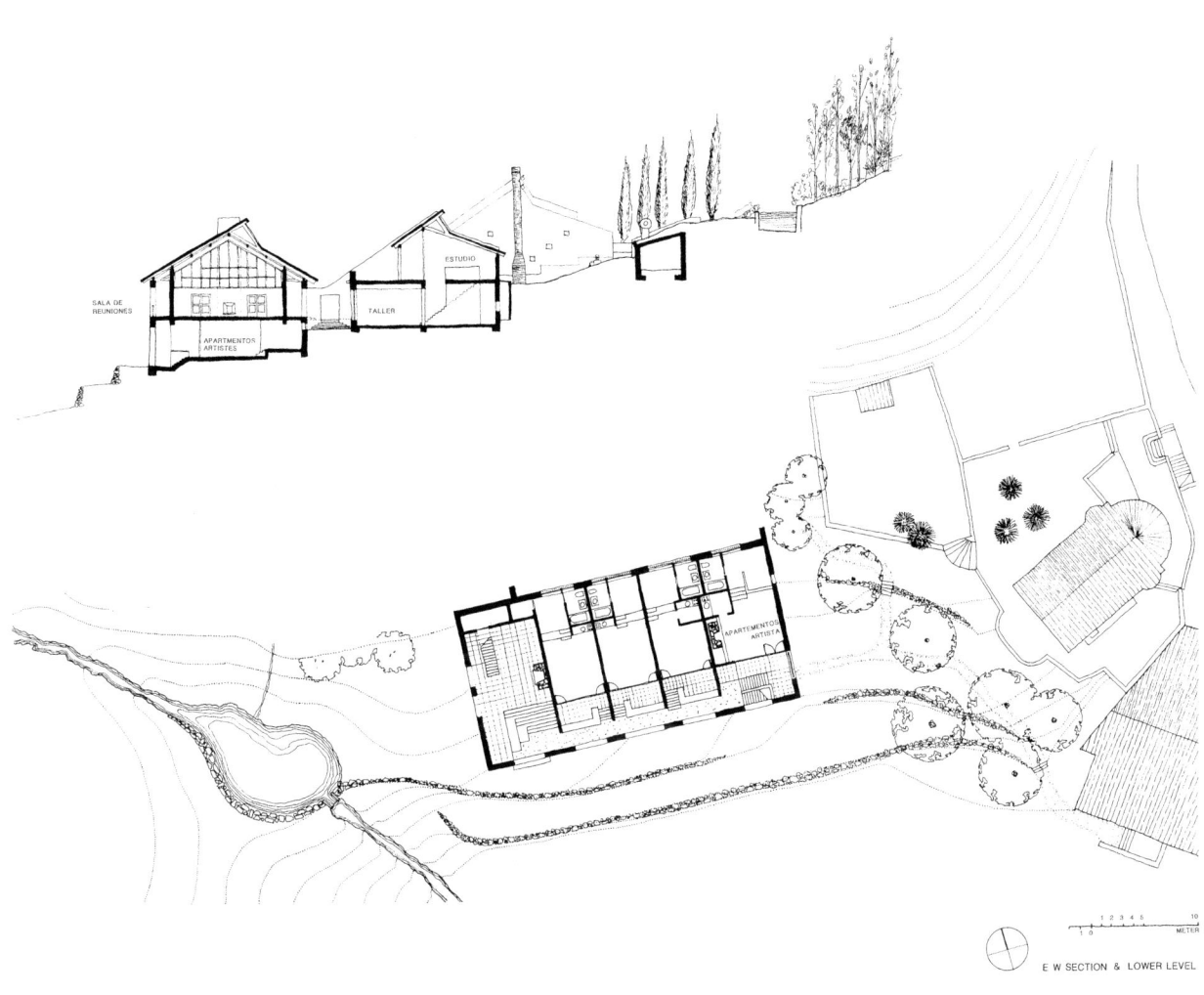

Artigas Foundation Studios, Barcelona, Spain _ SOM

Bishopsgate Project, Broadgate Phase 11
London, England 1988 – 1992

The London Broadgate Development is a 12-acre site spanning the railway tracks of Liverpool Station. The development includes office, trading floors, and retail. Of the 14 phased buildings, most are designed in a postmodern style recalling the materials and elements of traditional London buildings. The one exception is Phase 11, the only building to straddle the train tracks, requiring a structurally innovative solution that would best express itself architecturally. This is why Bruce Graham sent Brigitte, a diehard modernist, to London to design the project. Four parabolic steel arches create a bridge over the train tracks; from these arches hang the large, column-free office and trading floors. The building recalls the layout of the Inland Steel Building in Chicago with core functions, such as toilets rooms and exit stairs located in service towers at each end, freeing up the ground floor for an open transparency that reinforces the suspended structure.

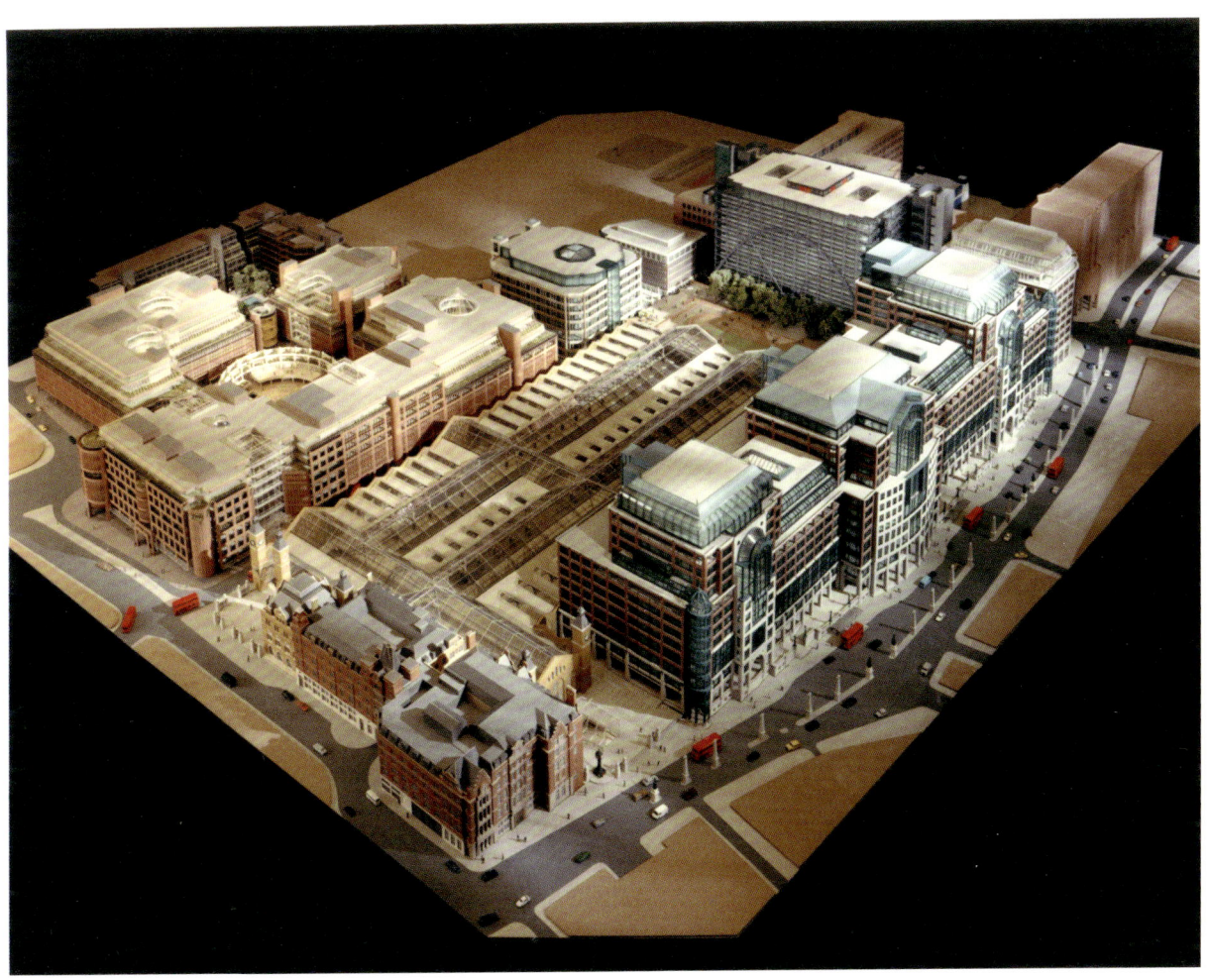

Broadgate Development Model _ SOM

Exchange House, Broadgate, London, England _ Alan Williams/SOM

Chapter—Work at SOM

Exchange House, Broadgate, London, England _ SOM

116 _ 117

WORK APART FROM SOM

Diakonie Housing

Kernen-Stetten, Germany 1965

Three multi-family residential buildings were designed for workers at the Diakonie. A simple concrete frame structure is expressed, with recessed balconies. A pedestrian bridge was designed to span a busy street and to connect the residences with other parts of the Diakonie.

Diakonie Worker Housing, Kernen-Stetten, Germany _ Author

Diakonie Pedestrian Bridge, Kernen-Stetten, Germany _ Author

House for Her Parents

Kernen-Stetten, Germany 1966

When Brigitte's father Ludwig retired as director of the Diakonie, he had to abandon the residence that the Diakonie had provided for him and his family. Brigitte was asked to design a new house for her parents to be located near the Diakonie, where his son, and Brigitte's brother, Peter took over as director. The house is a two-storey exposed concrete frame with clear glass windows set back from the frame for solar control. The main level contains the living quarters for Brigitte's parents. The half-submerged lower level contains bedrooms for Brigitte and other visitors.

House for Ludwig and Elisabeth Schlaich, Kernen-Stetten, Germany _ Author

House for Ludwig and Elisabeth Schlaich, Kernen-Stetten, Germany _ Wilfried Dechau

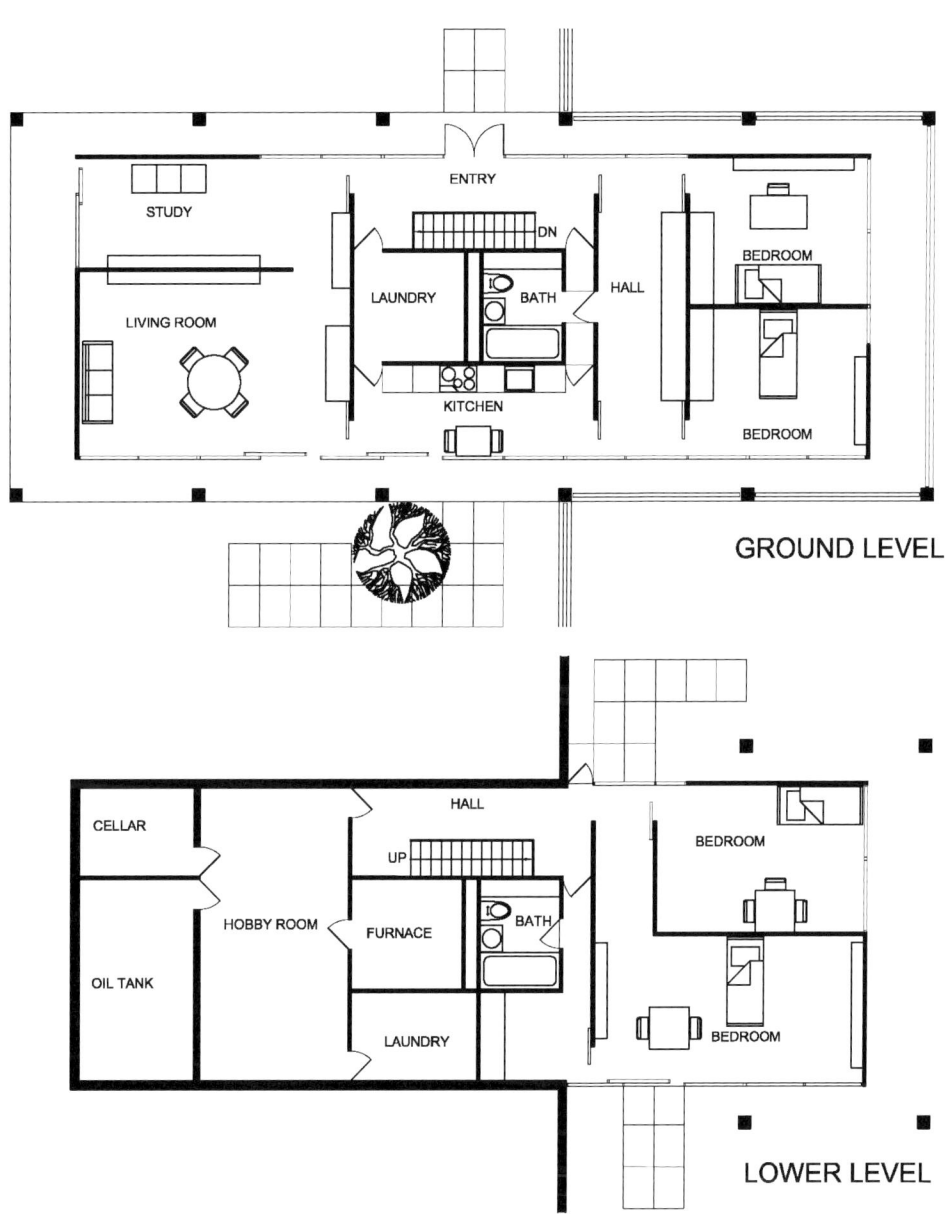

Chapter—Work apart from SOM

Jörg Schlaich Family Residence
Kernen-Stetten, Germany 1969

This house was designed for Brigitte's brother, his wife, and their four children. Due to its location near a school with a sloped roof, the local building authorities insisted that the house have a sloped roof. The exceedingly economical construction is of concrete masonry walls with wood floor and roof framing. The lowest level on the steep hillside is poured in place concrete. This level has a large circular window, a feature repeated in the Steinkopfstrasse Residence in Stuttgart. Brigitte's brother Jörg was the contractor and builder.

Jörg Schlaich House, Kernen-Stetten, Germany _ Wilfried Dechau

Jörg Schlaich House, Kernen-Stetten, Germany _ Wilfried Dechau

Chapter—Work apart from SOM

Jörg Schlaich House, Kernen-Stetten, Germany_ Wilfried Dechau

Jörg Schlaich House, Kernen-Stetten, Germany_ Wilfried Dechau

Chapter—Work apart from SOM

Steinkopfstrasse Residence
Stuttgart, Germany 1989

Brigitte's brother Jörg Schlaich purchased an investment property on a steep hillside in Stuttgart with panoramic views of the city. Brigitte was charged with designing a new multi-family residence there, including a garden apartment for herself to live in. In a radical break with the style of Mies and SOM, she designed a building with more of an influence from Le Corbusier and other European architects, as represented at the Stuttgart Weissenhofsiedlung housing estate of 1927. Mies was the director of that development, but this was early in his career, and the style of the buildings was more influenced by the De Stijl movement. Brigitte had also been one of his first students to see that Mies' designs were not as mathematically logical as most thought, and that he often made exceptions to the module. At street level is a one-level apartment with a two-level apartment above, the upper unit having open roof terraces. Brigitte's own garden apartment is nestled in the lower level of the sloping site.
A signature circular window, as used in the earlier Jörg Schlaich Family Residence, is the main focus of the garden apartment. But the most interesting, and least Miesian, feature of the complex is a unique silo shaped structure containing a spiral staircase which connects all of the levels.

Steinkopfstrasse Residence _ Wilfried Dechau

Steinkopfstrasse Residence _ Wilfried Dechau

Steinkopfstrasse Residence _ Wilfried Dechau

Chapter—Work apart from SOM

Steinkopfstrasse Residence _ Wilfried Dechau

Max-Eyth-See Pedestrian Bridge
Stuttgart, Germany 1989

Brigitte consulted with her brother, structural engineer Jörg Schlaich, on this suspension bridge over the river Neckar near the Max-Eyth-See recreation park in Stuttgart. On one side of the river are steep vineyards and on the other side lies a flat wooded area. Because of the unsymmetrical topography of the site, it was originally thought that a single mast would best represent this asymmetry, but further study showed that a single mast would be substantially taller than two masts. By concealing the park side mast in a grove of trees and by exposing the vineyard side mast, the proper relationship of each mast to its setting was achieved. The pedestrian approach to each end of the bridge was also designed to be sympathetic to each side's topography. On the vineyard side, the bridge deck curves away from the mast, and on the park side the bridge deck splits into two parts on either side of its mast. The curved design of the bridge deck was an engineering challenge that resulted in a fine balance of forms and forces.

Max-Eyth-See Bridge, Stuttgart, Germany _ Sibylle Schlaich

Chapter—Work apart from SOM

Max-Eyth-See Bridge, Stuttgart, Germany _ Sibylle Schlaich

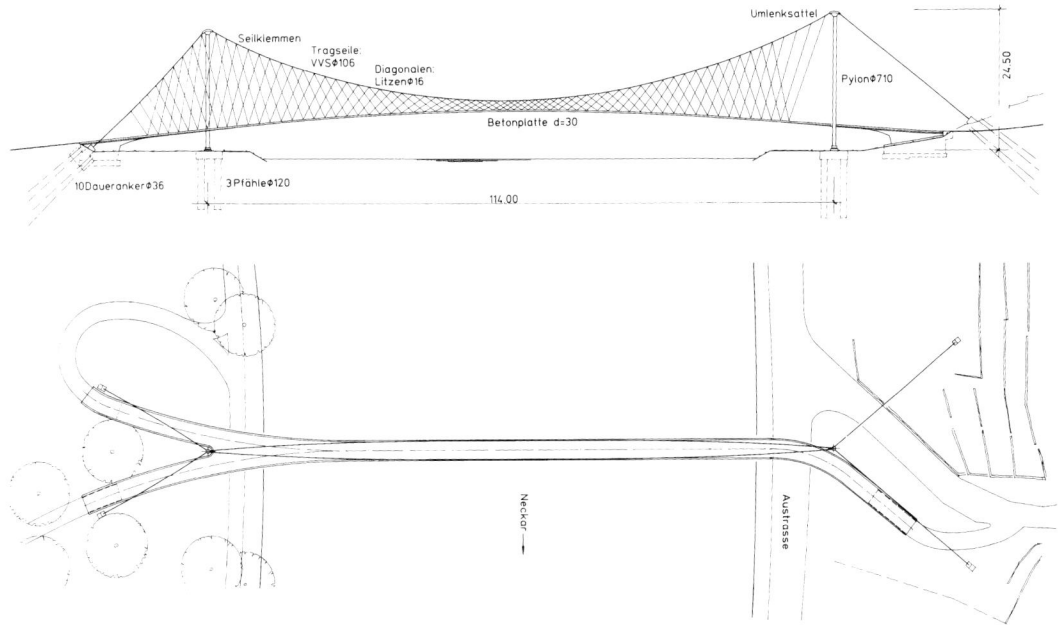

Technical Drawing _ schlaich bergermann partner

Sibylle Schlaich Residence
Berlin, Germany 1999

Sibylle, sister to Mike and Frieder, bought with her family a complex of buildings in Berlin's Mitte to serve as residence for her family as well as for her sister Anne, and to serve as offices for her and her husband's separate graphic design practices. Brigitte worked with Sibylle and her husband, Alexander Branczyk, on interior renovations as well as the outdoor garden areas.

EINGANGSBEREICH

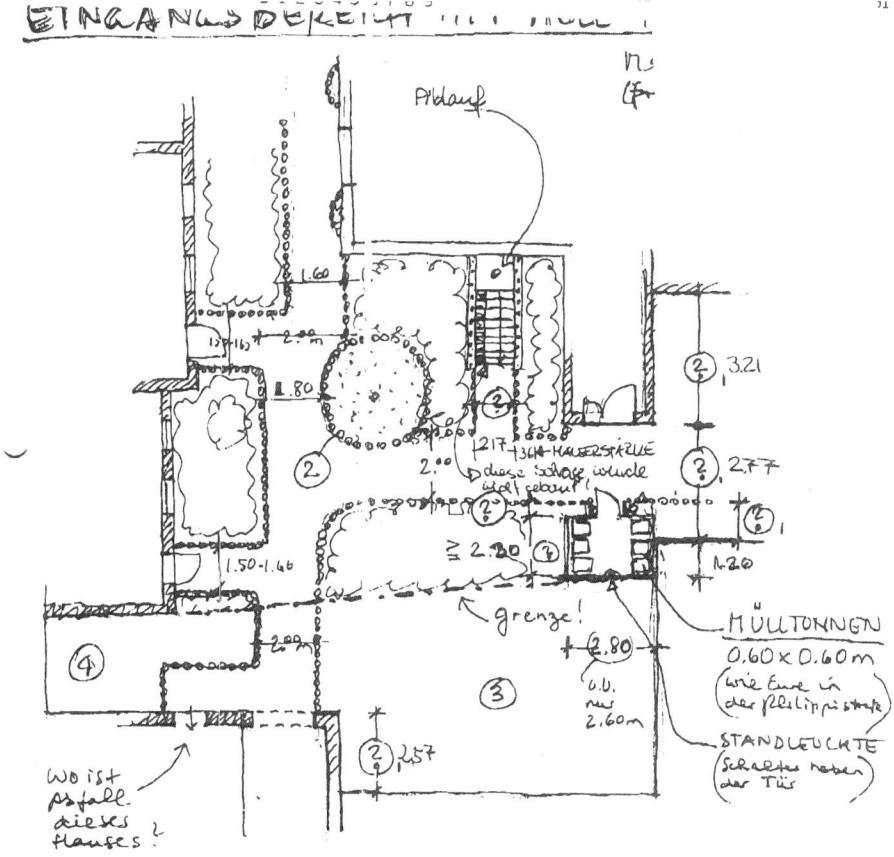

FRAGEN / HINWEISE:

① Bitte alle Maßlinien mit ? nachmessen u. eintragen.

② Wie groß soll dieser Kreis sein?

③ Dieser Teil nicht unter unserer Kontrolle!

④ ebenfalls — wo ist Asfalt für dieses Hinterhaus??

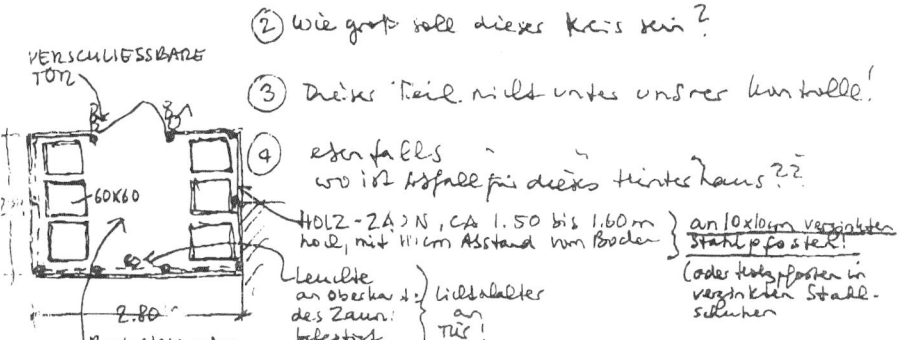

Frieder Schlaich Residence
Berlin, Germany 2009

After German reunification in 1991, several embassies in former East Berlin were vacated due to duplication with the West. Two of Brigitte's nephews, sons of Jörg Schlaich, bought two adjacent properties, the former Swiss embassy and the other, a vacant lot.
Mike Schlaich decided to build a new house on the vacant lot using infra-lightweight concrete, a material he had been pioneering with studies at his teaching post at the Technical University in Berlin. Frieder Schlaich chose to keep the existing structure and renovate it as a two-unit residential building. Brigitte worked with Frieder on the interior renovations and the addition of an exterior stair leading to the third-floor apartment.

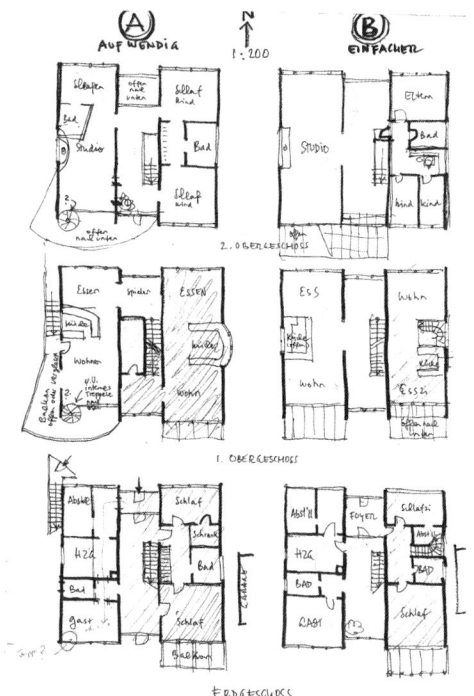

Frieder Schlaich Residence, Berlin, Germany _ Author

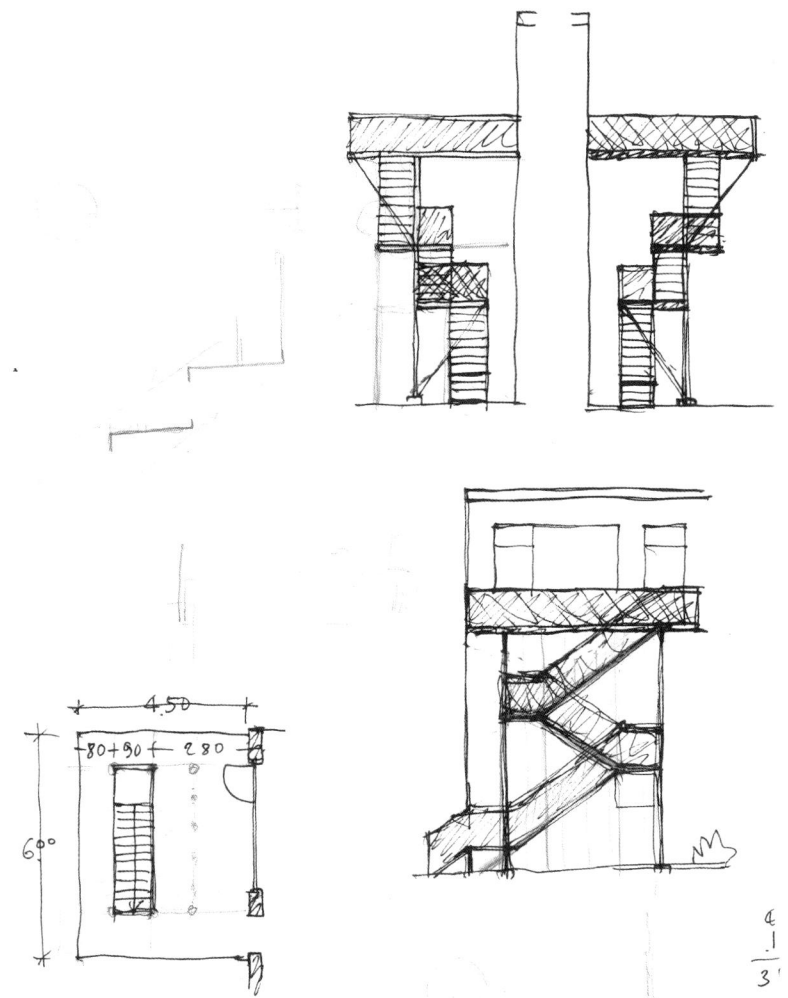

Frieder Schlaich Residence, Berlin, Germany _ Author

APPENDIX 1

Walter Peterhans and the Bauhaus

Walter Peterhans (1897–1960) was a teacher and course leader of photography at the Bauhaus from 1929 to 1933. In 1938, he immigrated to Chicago to teach the 'Visual Training' course to architecture students at Illinois Institute of Technology (IIT) under the direction of Mies van der Rohe. The course was so successful, it survived Peterhans by over 80 years and is the only course of the original Mies curriculum still being taught at IIT. At the Bauhaus, Peterhans' teaching involved using the theories of Kant, Plato, and Pythagoras to show how beauty is constructed in the mind, and how it can be created in works of art. Later in life, when Brigitte asked him about the Bauhaus, Walter responded, 'All that talk about the Bauhaus is coming out of my ears, it was just a school, you know.'

Peterhans' own work in the 1930s was close-up, still-life silver gelatin prints of everyday objects, meticulously composed using tweezers. In this time before colour photography, Peterhans' goal was to explore the ultimate in the precise detailing of halftones in black and white.

In addition to teaching at IIT (until 1960), he worked from 1945 to 1947 as a research associate for philosophy at the University of Chicago. In 1953, he was a guest lecturer at the Ulm School of Design (HfG), an influential school founded by Inge Scholl, former member of the anti-Nazi White Rose Group. There he was the head of the first basic course to follow the pedagogical principles of the Bauhaus.

Dead Hare _ Walter Peterhans

APPENDIX 2

DIARY OF AN OCEAN VOYAGE: GERMANY TO CHICAGO

Author's Note: I am including here a diary of Brigitte's first trip to America, including a layover in New York City, arriving in Chicago and settling in, and the beginning of her education at IIT.

On board the *MS Berlin*, Sunday, 9 September 1956
Today is already the sixth day on board, and since we are supposed to arrive in New York on Friday, we have already completed half our great voyage. A pity! You can't imagine a more lazy and comfortable life. But I'll tell the story one step after the other, so as not to forget anything.

So, after the somewhat very hectic final travel preparations at home, (will I never manage it otherwise?) the farewell at Stuttgart train station, at least for me, was mainly accompanied by a general breathlessness and the feeling of relief to have made it at least so far. It wasn't until the train left that I realised that I was actually leaving for a whole year – and I would have loved to get off again. But, by then, the platform with Father Muschu and Lotte was already far gone. In the Ludwigsburg area, we finally got the idea to look around for a place to sit, and indeed, there was some. With Mother's good sandwiches and the wonderful grapes and peaches, I recovered quite quickly, and in Mühlacker (we just sped through), I thought of my brother with mixed feelings, who – if he had known – would surely have stood at the platform and waved (?!?). I had to change trains in Wiesbaden and had some time for a little stroll through the city. From there, it went by express train on the right bank of the Rhine (I had never been on that side) until we reached Bad Honnef. The train was already full of Fulbrighters, who had all nicely labelled their suitcases with large slips of paper from Fulbright and Hapag Lloyd. Fortunately, I had not yet done so. Honnef is a typical, perhaps a second-class Rhine town. We had to report to the tourist office, received our accommodation slips there, and then marched there immediately to get rid of the luggage. The landlady of the *Deutsches Haus*, a genuine Rhinelander woman of 77 years with the temperament of a 35-year-old, had the house full of Fulbrighters. I ended up in a room with a blonde Berliner, who showed me all her jewellery the very first morning, including her evening, cocktail, and other dresses, her *Petitkötchen*, blouses, and flared suits. Her father's name is Richard, but he's called Ulf, the two brothers are Wulf and Wolfram, she has a penchant for cats, black with yellow eyes, etc., etc. But I had to go straight to the Kurhaus for the opening of the conference! I was dead tired and would much rather have lain down, but I didn't dare do anything else because everyone rushed there so eagerly. A considerable crowd had gathered In the large hall of the Kurhaus, presumably the Kursaal, with coffee, cake, and significant speeches in English. An estimated 100–120 people were there, most of them between 20 and 30, about 10 per cent well-off, in their Stresemann suits, some of them lecturers or even professors, who were also going along. Fortunately, I soon approached a secretary, whom I told about my intended visit to the Soroptimists in Bonn in an appropriately significant manner. She revealed to me, in private and under the seal of secrecy, that the tickets would only be issued on Monday during the day, so practically nothing would happen before then. After a good dinner in the spa garden (nice cold cuts), while again everyone else gathered for even more introductory lectures, we took off until Monday, and after a short stroll, I fell dead tired into the not quite clean bed of the good Madame Eupen. On Sunday morning, all the house guests gathered around a sumptuous breakfast table, which made up amply for the dubious hygiene, in a splendidly kitschy furnished dining room with even more beautiful ancient family photos. On Saturday evening, I had called the former Soroptimist president of Bonn, the architect Wera Meyer-Waldeck, who immediately invited me to lunch for Sunday. There was still some time for that when we went to the train station via Bonn after breakfast, and because we heard the bells ringing as we passed the Protestant Church in Honnef, we went in. My last, truly Protestant church service for a year. The bells rang for a quarter of an hour, and the church got really crowded. The sermon didn't make the biggest impression on me. There was a long liturgy, the confession of faith, a lot of singing, etc. Anyway, despite the short sermon, the whole service lasted quite long. Meyer-Waldeck is an architect and lives in a terraced house in a quite nice federal civil servants' housing estate, built around 1950 by one of the Taut brothers.

At the time, she was working on the interior design of the Bundeshaus. The original version of the large plenary hall, the workrooms of the Federal President, the Chancellor, and the restaurant etc. are her doing. However, she did not blame me for not knowing that her name was completely unknown to me. She studied with Gropius at the Bauhaus and graduated there under Mies. Now she works for the *Bauausstellung* ('Berlin Building Exhibition' of 1957), on the projects called 'Apartment of Tomorrow'. She is a spirited little reddish-blonde lady, with a somewhat unshapely form, hardly interesting looking, but in the long run more and more likeable because of her very agile intelligence and sense of humour. Without a doubt an industrious person, but not in an unpleasant way. Her apartment has quite a nice, not-too-small kitchen downstairs and a larger living room (the usual terrace house layout) with a pretty little residential garden, an upstairs bathroom, a small bedroom, and two office rooms. It is furnished very simply and without the extravagance often common among our kind, but quite cosy. She served a cultivated lunch she had fabricated herself with the assistance of her young co-worker, who was also invited, and the entertainment was a roaring one. Not so much about the Soroptimists, for whom I had actually come here – but what should I always ask? – than about all sorts of things, above all architecture. She was born in Egypt, grew up in Europe, worked after the war first as a lecturer in Dresden, where she was fired, then in England, and at some point also for a few months in the US as a delegate. Of course, she has the best connections there, knows pretty much all the good architects personally, Frank Lloyd Wright, Neutra, Wurster, Mies, and Gropius, of course, etc. She told me that if I needed to know anything or needed any help, I should just contact her, she would help, and that I should make use of the American Soroptimists wherever I could. They had an enormous sphere of influence in the States. After washing up together, my visit extended beyond coffee, and I was sitting on pins and needles, because I had arranged to meet Friedrich at the Bonn train station, and the time had long since passed. Afterwards, Madame sent me to the current Bonn Soroptimist president, Dr. Roters, a psychologist and career counsellor at the Bonn employment office. There, I should get some reading materials about the club. To be on the safe side and not to get stuck for another couple of hours, I took F. with me this time and regretted that I had not done the same before, because it went well and was very nice. Nevertheless, it was too late for our planned Rhine tour back to Honnef. Following a small city stroll, all the ship stations had already closed. So, we dined in Bonn and took the Rheinuferbahn home. In the Kurhaus zu Honnef, the evening events seemed to be coming to an end.

Monday, 10 September 1956
We did not show ourselves again until the next morning and, as we were assured from all sides, did not seem to have missed anything. After a last lecture on the refugee problem in Germany by an appropriate Bonn ministerial, or similar official, the actual travel information began. After dully waiting around, I finally managed to get my tickets around 4:00 p.m. You can't imagine how dumb most of the Fulbrighters are, what a bunch of people that was! Most of the scholarship holders have only a travel scholarship, i.e. they go on their own account for a year or have a scholarship from somewhere else (such as the theologians from the World Council of Churches, there are quite a few of them, among others a counsellor of Peter – name? A funny little guy, the nephew of Aunt Florentine, etc.) (or a scholarship from the DAAD or a partial scholarship, which they got through their own connections from some American college) as a real complete Fulbrighter, including me, a total of only 36 guys are going this year (in contrast to always at least 120–180), and you can really consider it a small miracle that it worked out for me and even more so as desired to Mies in Chicago. In total, there are five architects this year, two are in our transport, the others already at the end of August. There are about 100 people in our transport, a few professors and lecturers and a few older gentlemen among them. Some even with their spouses, but they have to pay for them themselves.
But I have to cut this short, as otherwise I'll need three more days. So, we started Monday evening in Honnef with buses to the Bonn main station. Everything was over organised. You only had to trot along with the bunch and received even more tickets, the hand luggage was even taken and stowed in the train, in reserved compartments, a foolproof procedure. Departure, Bonn at 10:12 p.m. I hardly slept during the trip, contrary to my normal habits. In Bremen, it was just getting light.

After a hearty breakfast, further luggage, and other formalities, we still had an hour until the departure of the special train of *Berlin* passengers to Bremerhaven. I, of course, quickly ran to the center, the very beautiful square with the cathedral and city hall, the *Roland* statue, the *Town Musicians of Bremen*, and many other fantastic old buildings. Unfortunately, it was much too short. On the way through an area that reminded me very much of our visit to Holland a year ago, there were a few real Westphalian farms to see, with their timber-framed houses and large, in part, thatched roofs. Other than that, I was just dog-tired.
We saw Bremerhaven only in passing, probably no loss, because the destination of the special train, the Columbus Quai, lies even a bit further, directly at the water's edge and directly at the ship. It went altogether very quickly. I could just post the postcards to you before we were shuffled through the boarding bridges in a dense crowd onto the *Berlin*. The crowd in the narrow corridors there was huge, with the stewards and stewardesses playing traffic guards. I quickly found my cabin and left the blue bag and satchel there (suitcase again came automatically) to get back on the open deck as quickly as possible. With the brightest weather and a lot of blaring of sentimental music from the ship's band, we finally left at 12:00 noon sharp. A huge crowd stood at the pier (no wonder there was such a crowd on board before, as nearly everyone had been accompanied by people who quickly wanted to look at the ship's interior) and said goodbye more or less spiritedly. We Fulbrighters also had many relatives there, but I was actually glad that none of you were there. Such a ship farewell is cruel. First, all non-passengers have to disembark, though they still linger at the pier for hours, you can still see each other, but you can only talk by yelling over the 20-metre distance. Everything is waving, scarves and coloured ribbons, and shouting. Finally, the ship starts to move, very slowly. The distance gets bigger and bigger, the music finally becomes sentimental, it takes at least another quarter of an hour until we finally see each other only like dots in the distance, and then not at all. I am with three other Fulbright or half-Fulbright girls together in the cabin. A-deck and pretty much midship. It's pretty good. We even have a hatch we are allowed to open in decent weather, which is quite nice to do despite the air conditioning. Most tourist-class cabins don't have a porthole, so no daylight either. Despite its small

size, such a cabin is quite comfortable (see sketch). We lie in comfortable bunk beds on top of each other, two of us to a closet, and each has large drawers. Everything is spotlessly clean, every day the snow-white towels, which are still from the Swedish era of the ship, with three woven crowns (the same sign also on cutlery, etc.), are changed, the beds are made up twice every day, that is, if you lie down sometime during the day, and already yesterday the sheets were changed (!). The steward does everything for you. You can take a bath as often as you want. I do this regularly in the morning at 6:30 a.m., because I always wake up so early with the clock being constantly reset, and you're always in bed for 10–12 hours daily. The stewardess knocks for me when she has already run the bath. Soap and sponge and also daily fresh large bath towels are ready. Everything completely free of charge, i.e. included in the fare (approximately 850 Deutschmarks (DM) per crossing). In addition, there is, also free of charge, an indoor swimming pool with a sauna, gymnastics room, etc. There again are towels and everything, only the deck chairs on the open deck have to be rented extra, 10 DM, for the whole trip, with a cushion and a thick wool blanket. I got mine on the top deck, and there you lie around for half the day, reading, sleeping, talking more or less, getting up to play a bit of shuffleboard (a funny game where you take turns in two parties to shoot plate-sized wooden discs into a number field or push them with long sticks) or to look for dolphins or whales or ships (all very rare, at intervals of about two days!).

It is unbelievable how fast time passes, although one actually does practically nothing the whole day. Today, we've been underway already for almost eight days. (In the meantime, it's now Tuesday, 11 September.) Until now, we have had quite decent weather, much sunshine, although rarely, except for this morning, a wind force of more than 3–9 and 'rough' sea. The *Berlin*, because she is so heavy (an advantage of her old and solid construction), lies excellently on the water, even today, when we had a wind force of at least 10 and so-called high seas. Nevertheless, everyone was glad to have escaped the hurricane, which was approaching quite threateningly, by changing course, after all portholes, hatches, and bulkheads had already been closed last night, the necessary bags and preventive tablets distributed everywhere, and great rumours circulated among the passengers. Enough people got seasick as it was – at dinner, some tables were quite sparsely occupied – and the happily spared didn't necessarily want to take on extreme tests of strength, where you are then supposed to fly out of bed, get the plates in your lap, and always know where up and down is. As I said, the *Berlin* is no longer the youngest, but it is a very dignified ship through and through. For that, one gladly accepts her slowness. There are about 950 passengers, 200 in first class, the rest tourists. In between, there is nothing. Plus, the crew, about 350 people. So, most of the ship belongs to the tourist-class passengers, where it's supposed to be much more entertaining than in the *blasé* first class anyway. We have a large dining room down in the belly at the same level as the fabulous galley and first-class dining room. There, we eat in two shifts, I am in the second 'session'. You always sit at the same tables with the same table steward. Food plays quite a role, and if you look at the enclosed menus you will understand. Everyone can eat what they want and as much as they want, only liquor has to be paid extra. I think I have gained at least 10 pounds, but also never in my life have I had such feasts three times a day for 10 days. Breakfast is still the greatest! In addition, there is coffee and cake in the afternoon and in the evening at 10:00 p.m. sandwiches on huge platters, in each of the various social rooms, where you can, depending on your mood, read in the library, smoke in the smoking room, flirt and drink in the tavern, listen to music and dance in the ballroom, talk or play (prize and other games) in the game room, play the piano somewhere else, or write again somewhere else. There is also a cinema, dance lessons, table tennis, slide shows (partly on the initiative of the passengers), and extra amusement among the Fulbright students, where individual talents emerge bit by bit – singing in choirs, reciting comic poems, etc. Every evening there is an extra party and a special event. A welcome ball, a Bavarian evening, to which everyone who could came dressed in *Dirndl* and *Lederhosen* and where there were *Weißwürste*, *Radi*, etc. and the corresponding performances, *Winzerfest* (the same in Rhineland). There is always something going on, and you could easily go out every evening. Fortunately, I managed to stay away from everything until now, and when I did go out, I didn't stay longer than 11.00 p.m., which is usually 10:00 p.m. because the clock is set back one hour every second night. So, at the moment, when I'm lying in the bathtub at 6:30 a.m., it's already 11:30 a.m. with you, and Muschu is already thinking about what to cook today.

The main language on the *Berlin* is German. The crew is all German, and that is supposed to be much better than a mixed crew from all over the world, like on the *United States*. They are all very proud of their ship, starting with the smallest ship's boy, who is always terribly important and looks like a 12 year old. Most passengers are also Germans or German-Americans who are returning from a long visit to Germany and have therefore brushed up on their German. Funny are also their children, who now also speak some German (depending) but otherwise almost all are horribly ill-bred and bully everything, but no one risks to say anything to them.

Travelogue: Arrival in New York and Chicago, Sept. / Oct. 1956
It was in fact a minor hurricane our *Berlin* passed a few days before the American shore. I don't remember exactly how much I mentioned about it in the first report. On the last day at sea and on the very last morning while entering New York, we had brilliant weather, and you came to regret that this wonderfully lazy life should now come to an end. You had just got so used to it. On top of that, we were still very busy on the last day with preparations for the 'talent evening'. Together with a Berlin student, I prepared a ghastly *moritat* (a street ballad), which another Fulbright Fellow sang. We had a lot of fun with it. The main events of the second-to-last day were the increasingly frequent encounters with other ships, even fishing boats. While out on the Atlantic, you almost never saw anything, strange when most ships choose exactly the same path, the shortest one. At sunset, a fabulous one, we passed the fire boat *Nontaget*, a little ship that always lies in the same place with a crew of about eight men. They were standing on deck altogether and waving. The collision of the *Andrea Doria* happened very close to there.
On the very last morning, we got up insanely early, hoping to see a picturesque sunrise over the sea from the first glimmer of light. It was still pitch black, and when it started to dawn, after about an hour and a half, we were disappointed to see nothing of the sun. But soon, we saw the first sliver of land, a narrow grey strip on the port side to the right. That was Long Island.
Not much happened for quite a long time after that. We were busy enough packing, exchanging addresses (I'm missing the address of a Dr. Hafter or something who

Chapter—Appendix

went to New Jersey. I wrote it down on the back of a menu, and it might have ended up with one of you. Please check. And send it quickly!), and eating as much as possible at breakfast, and an early lunch – not so easy in the light fever of joy and excitement for New York, etc. The 'tipping' of the various stewards and waiters also played a big role. Whoever thinks of starting a sea voyage of the same magnitude soon, make a note: table steward, five dollars, cabin steward, three to four dollars, and stewardess (this applies especially to females, who have more to do with it) about two to three dollars, depending. You can skip the deck steward if you like. Instead, you'd better give something to one or other of the little ship's boys, pardon, elves who are always so terribly eager and delighted to receive a tip.
Entering the harbour of New York – it's best to read about it in a good travel book – we didn't have the most beautiful weather. It was sunny and hot, but quite hazy, so you could see the shores on the right and left, which were slowly getting closer and closer, and then finally split into two arms, Manhattan as a bizarre silhouette between them, with many details, the houses, cars, and trees, but not very vivid. Likewise, then the first skyscrapers. Therefore, to me at least, they didn't seem so insane. Certainly, and unfortunately, you're also kind of educated by the many exaggerated and dramatising colour shots of them. Only from very close up, when you already have the green-patinised Lady of Liberty behind you on the left and immediately after that you also(?) start to pass Manhattan, only to dock somewhere further back, on its left side, just at that moment it is already overwhelming, this artificial stone mountain range. Everyone was taking photos like crazy the whole time – a popular saying: 'if you had all the money that has been spent on photos over the years at such a moment!' I heard it at least 10 times. All in all, such a harbour entrance takes hours. We also lay for a while without moving. Everyone on deck, of course. Pilot boat. Other ships. Buoys carrying melodiously sounding bells! Helicopters, gondolaing over the water at the same height as you, cosy old-fashioned looking ferries for passenger transport between the various islands and peninsulas of the giant city. Then you got the first mail, even before you saw Manhattan, somehow delivered from the land. I also got two letters and later in the harbour more mail – a welcome change in the more than boring endless standing around at the various

passport and other controls that came on board and that you had to pass before you were even allowed to set foot on this promised land. We Fulbrighters received a hotel address, a ticket for the onward journey, and another stack of beautiful brochures about everything America has to offer. Well-organised. After all, this wasn't the first time at it. More waiting. The luggage had to be all taken off first, because afterward, every passenger had to go through customs with all their stuff. Letter by letter, everyone lined up in a large hall. I put my small suitcase next to my old trunk (decidedly the best piece in the bunch), grabbed a customs officer who was standing around waiting, and, after opening both lids slightly, I was done. He could see my lack of possessions. Now all I had to do was to pass through the barrier with both suitcases together with the help of a free luggage carrier, hand over the trunk there, go to the transport company already notified and paid for, etc. from the ship, which transported it to my departure station (there, I also only had to request it verbally on the day of the onward journey, to finally receive it at the station in Chicago and transport it home by taxi. I recommend this method to everyone. Costs all in all approximately –DM, from Stuttgart main station, and you don't have to do anything yourself!). Then I was free for New York as one of the first off the whole ship, as Günther confirmed, who suddenly stood before me behind the last barrier. A great surprise! I hadn't expected to see him at all. It was a reunion, for the first time after almost exactly two years! Back when he left Genoa for the US on the *Independence*. It was late afternoon before we found our hotel (not far from the Empire State Building), booked our rooms on the 16th floor, and could finally start our first stroll through New York. The streets were surprisingly quiet and traffic-free. I had imagined it differently, but over the weekend, Manhattan is always nearly deserted, only to be pure traffic chaos on the other days. I experienced this enough on the following Monday. We walked down to the United Nations building on the East River. The administration tower's huge glass façade reflected picturesque sunset clouds. The massive UN facility was also deserted and inaccessible. We had something to eat in one of the countless, more or less nice bar restaurants, where one usually gets some drinks, sandwiches, the obligatory 'hamburgers' (meat patties made out of chopped meat), and other quick meals slapped down in front of us, the bill too (not cheap the

stuff), which one pays at a cash register at the exit. I had to think of Erlebacher's. I'm no longer surprised by their lack of pretensions. In every respect! It's funny how, in this country, the highest perfection is mixed with striking primitiveness, and that in every 'sector'. But perhaps that is precisely why such top performances are achieved, because, on the other hand, people do without a lot of things or don't value them at all, or don't even know about them. Of course, these are all preliminary impressions and statements. I should actually abstain from making them after such a short time. Even though I have been in the country for almost six weeks now. This America is so oversized and overwhelmingly immense and, in my opinion, at least as different from Europe (let alone Germany) as Turkey is, for example, where it is impossible to have and give valid impressions after a few weeks' time. There are department stores here where you can buy everything. Their floor space is on average five to 15 times as big as that of the Stuttgart Union, for example, but there are twice as many floors. You can easily get lost in these places. If you stand in the middle of one of these floors, you can't see the outer walls (the 'horizon') and it's an art to find your way out. The choice is overwhelming, and with all the variations, you can't make a decision, or you rarely find something you really like, and when you have found a cheap but beautiful earthenware dish, for example, and would like to find someone to serve you, you may spend half an hour rushing around in vain until one of the ladies finally deigns to take your order. In the meantime, she keeps running away, and it turns out you can't even see samples or at least pictures of all the items you want, so you have to risk buying randomly.
Back to New York: in the evening, when it was dark and we were tired from all the walking around, we sat in the charming, brightly lit garden courtyard of Rockefeller Center. That's a great thing. The next morning, we went on a guided tour of this skyscraper complex. I don't remember exactly, but 50,000 to 80,000 people work in these six or eight skyscrapers, all connected underground, built according to a general plan in the last 20–25 years (look it up in an encyclopedia). And how the stuff is built! Solid, with the best materials and also quite convincing from our architectural point of view. It's a city in itself, and apart from a church and yet another special weirdness, there's everything in it that a city otherwise contains. From the roof of

the highest building (65th floor, not quite as high as the Empire State Building) we had a great view at the end. Weather not quite clear, though, but sunny, a boiling heat (like we haven't had all summer), really humid.

New York is understandably often compared to Istanbul. The location is very similar, an estuary opening into a wide bay, with various arms, canals, offshore islands, etc. The wide islands, peninsulas, and the sea are all very different. The widely branching islands, peninsulas, etc. in between are all quite high, and mountainous. And everywhere everything densely built-up. But, unlike in New York, Istanbul's streets and alleys run in medieval (or even earlier) irregularity, quite chaotic in places, but absolutely charming and picturesque-romantic. In New York, there are practically only right angles, streets drawn with a ruler, a grid(?) in which the longitudinal streets have names, the transverse ones only numbers (with exceptions). The only *enfant terrible* is Broadway – you have to accept its special position, which are the most important and interesting – which unabashedly runs diagonally through the middle of this system and ends up at the very bottom of the southern tip of the island in old Manhattan, where the streets also run crookedly and diagonally. On Broadway, the streets are called West – on the left – and East – on the right – and an address, such as 531 E. 71 St., is easily found at number 531, East of Broadway at 71st Street. An address such as 456 Madison Avenue (I forgot, the north-south ones are avenues, the east-west ones are streets) at the corresponding number on Madison Avenue. In Chicago, this system is not quite as easy to understand, but once you get the hang of it, it's basically just as foolproof. There, too, all streets are almost exclusively right-angled, but since the extension to both sides, or to all four sides, is even more endless than in Manhattan, which is at least halfway bounded by water, two axes were introduced to separate east from west and north from south. They meet in the city, called the 'Loop' or Downtown, the south-north streets are again the Avenues with real names mostly, the west-east streets have numbers and are called Streets. So our address, 3101 S. Wabash Avenue, is called house number 01 in the 31st block southbound on Wabash Avenue, where the 31st block is the section of the street between the intersection of Wabash Avenue with 31st Street and the intersection of Wabash Avenue with 32nd Street. You start counting with 01 as the house number at the 31st intersection, and there are never more than 99 houses until the next intersection, i.e. block. So, if you should suddenly find yourself in Chicago, you should almost be able to find your way around.

In the middle of the sea of stone that is Manhattan, a huge rectangle has been cut out: Central Park. Unfortunately, I don't have a New York map with a scale on it, and estimating anything in this giant city is almost impossible for our European sense of scale. The length of a block, which we might calculate at 100 m based on the number of buildings and our habits, is certainly at least twice that, because each building is several times larger than we know them. Central Park is certainly three to four km long and almost one km wide (if the generally accepted rule: eight blocks = one mile is correct for there, then it would even be six km long and correspondingly wider), has huge lakes, and if you want to see it, please walk up to my room, where it hangs on the board behind the drawing table. From the Rockefeller Center roof garden, we could also see the two main centres of New York-Manhattan, recognisable by the clustering of particularly tall skyscrapers. The first center, Southern Manhattan, is located at the tip of the island, facing the Atlantic, as has been mentioned many times before. The second center is grouped around Rockefeller Center. The houses in between are 'low-rise', if you want to call 12–20 storeys that. The streets are narrow canyons, even if they are as wide as Königsstraße. Stately churches (of the noblest neo-architecture) are completely hidden. Typical for this city – also for Chicago – are the strange cylindrically shaped (height about the same diameter) water reservoirs above all the roofs and the bizarre assemblies of the countless iron fire escapes on every house. I'll have to take pictures of both sometime. It's hard to describe.

From Rockefeller Center we marched to the famous Lever House (famous for architects. Jörg has two photos of it hanging in his room). It actually looks even better, and it looks new, although it's already six years old. It was done by the architectural team Skidmore, Owings & Merrill, who also designed the American consulates in Stuttgart and Frankfurt, which is obvious. Skidmore, Owings & Merrill have, as far as I know, the largest architectural firm in the world, at least 250–300 employees. I was there once. It's the purest factory: a huge room – the whole ninth floor of a large commercial building – with about 150 drawing stations. In long rows, one behind the other. Opposite the Lever House, Mies van der Rohe is building a large commercial building, the Seagram Building. Also, an all-glass façade. That will be a special corner for New York! The first 10 or 12 floors were already erected, steel construction of course. Finally, we went to the Museum of Modern Art to see a special exhibition on 'Textiles' and, of course, the permanent exhibition. They have beautiful things there. I definitely have to go there again. Among others, there are some famous Rousseaus, Modiglianis, and Klees . Because it was pouring down afterward, with the most humid temperature, we had no choice but to go to the cinema. Nothing bad, by the way. The English colour film *Moby Dick* based on the famous Herman Melville novel. A seafaring story with the mysterious white whale at its center. Excellent shots, mostly intentionally somewhat overexposed and underlining the mystical atmosphere in their pale colours. The whole film takes place practically only on the ocean, on a sailing ship. (Without any … being). A nocturnal stroll around Times Square, with breathtaking neon advertising (everything flashes and moves in all colours. Ribbons of lettering racing criss-cross. Huge men's heads emitting real curls of smoke advertising a brand of cigarettes…insane). Underneath, a dense collection of the craziest guys I've ever seen. Indescribable get-ups, especially of the females. You feel like you're in the most fantastic film. People in expensive evening dresses, beggars in between – Whites, Blacks, and Asians – and all mixtures thereof. My mouth was open the whole time.

On Sunday, we walked down to Southern Manhattan through completely deserted streets. Endlessly. At least 10 km. Maybe more. Wall Street was deserted (one bank next to the other, where millions are stacked up and the world's business is done). The architecture was all the more monumental. Great. The street itself is narrow, no wider than Fürstenstraße perhaps, and each building at least 30–50 storeys high. The sky is just a small, jagged spot, way up high, to which the eye climbs endless expanses of windows. But not 10 minutes from this imposing square, one suddenly feels transported to an alleyway in Beijing or Hong Kong. 'Chinatown'. Narrow streets with three-to-four-storey houses teeming with Chinese. Swarms of cute slit-eyed children with black heads of hair. Strange music. Almost only Chinese is spoken, in the shops almost only Chinese goods (strange vegetables, gruesome-looking dried fish, fresh fish. Chinese porcelain, baskets, kimonos, of course, also a lot of souvenir junk, because many foreigners come to this strange quarter), all house numbering and advertisements in Chinese characters. We walked around for a long time and finally fortified ourselves with a typical Chinese chopstick meal, chop suey, sweet-and-sour carp with almonds, etc. and of course, rice.

On Monday morning, New York was transformed and became really N e w Y o r k. Such traffic! It takes hours to go a relatively short distance by bus. In some places, you can definitely walk faster. At every intersection, every 200 m, a stop light with endless waiting, plus a halt at every stop light. It's terrible. We saw the UN building from the inside with a guided tour – did you appreciate the special stamps (?) enough? The four small conference rooms, decorated differently by the architects of the different nations, and the large general assembly room. In the UN, 50 of the 58 people in the world can translate a foreign language into another language the second it is recorded. There are places in the conference halls where you can set a pointer to the language you want (English, French, Spanish, German, and one more I can't remember for sure) and get it translated absolutely in parallel with the proceedings, from the translators' booths, through a headset.

It's time to leave New York, otherwise I'll need many more pages and weeks. The day passed quickly with a visit to the Institute of International Education, for money, etc. The traffic was horrendous, as I said, and it took hours to get there. The New Yorkers made me green with envy, fabulously slim ladies in their best clothes, very tasteful and fancy shoes! Bags!

Günther left for Chicago by train in the afternoon. We exchanged our tickets because the train is faster and he had to go to the office, and because I could see much more from the bus. I used the time until the bus left in the evening and went up the Empire State Building, the tallest building in New York. Here, I had a great sunset with a thunderstorm coming up. The bus ride was very long and exhausting, almost 24 hours. I felt terribly sick in places. Despite all the comforts, a bus isn't the last(?) thing, you're so caged in and can never move around. Every few hours, there was a stop at some kind of rest area, and everybody rushed into the designated place. Most of the time, the rest stops were never in scenic places. One is also completely

s wird Zeit, dass wir New York verlassen, sonst brauche ich noch viele Seiten und Wochen. Der Tag verging vollends schnell mit Vorsprache beim Institute of International Education, wegen Geld usw. Der Verkehr war wie gesagt horrend und brauchte Stunden. Mich möchten die New-Yorkerinnen vor Neid erblassen! Sagenhaft schlanke Damen in bester Kleidung, sehr geschmackvoll und chicke Schuhe! Taschen!

Guenther fuhr schon nachmittags mit dem Zug ab nach Chicago, wir tauschten unsre Fahrkarten, weil der Zug schneller ist und er ins Buero musste und weil ich vom Bus aus viel mehr sehen konnte. Ich nuetze die Zeit bis zur Busabfahrt am Abend und fuhr aufs Empire-State-Bldg. rauf, dem hoechsten Gebaeude New Yorks. Hier hatte ich einen tollen Sonnenuntergang mit aufziehendem Gewitter. – – Die Busfahrt war sehr lange und anstrengend, fast 24 Stunden. Mir war stellenweise furchtbar schlecht, trotz allem Komfort ist ein Bus doch nicht das Letzte; man ist so eingesperrt und kann sich nie herumbewegen. Alle paar Stunden wurde an einer Art "Raststelle Halt" gemachtwo alles stuerzte in das hierfuer vorgesehene Lokal. Meist lagen ausgerechnet die Raststellen nie an landschaftlich schoenen Plaetzen. Man ist auch restlos eingesperrt an diesen Autobahn-Haltepunkten, ringsum Zaun. Die Fahrt ging durch endlose Felder, viel Mais, dazwischen kleine Waeldchen, einzelne grosse Baumgruppen, unter Ihnen dann meist die Farmen, mit den typischen, sehr kubisch wirkenden Schunen, oft dunkelrot gestrichen, einem hohen Siloturm (rund, mit silbrig-glaenzendem Kugeldeckel) und dem Wohnhaus in altmodischem en. 1. Landhausstil, meist 2-stockig, gestrichenes Holz.

Die Einfahrt in Chicago war toll. Zuerst durchfaehrt man die ganzen Schwerindustrie im Sueden scheusslich-schoen. Dann entlang dem See (Lake Shore Drive) ins Zentrum. Die Stadt ist denkbar bloede hingebaut. Die schoenste Seite, zum See hin ist fuer die Autos reserviert. Eine 6-fache Strasse entlang dem ganzen Ufer, aber meist nicht nahegenug um den See richtig sehn zu koennen. Rechts und links breite Gruenstreifen, parkaehnlich. – Ch. ist eine Riesenstadt, wahnsinnig ausgedehnt, meist nur 2-3 stockig bebaut, dazwischen grosse Strecken die fast voellig verslumt, verfallen sind und kaum noch bewohnt. Unser IIT (Illinois Institute of Technology) liegt auch mitten in so einer verlotterten Gegend. Man ist z.Zt. dabei, in einem langjaehrigen Programm, hier Ordnung zu schaffen. Die ganzen halb erfallenen, urspruenglich gar nicht so ueblen Haeuser werden der "eihe nach vollends geraeumt (manchmal fragt man sich wirklich, ob in diesen Loechern ueberhaupt noch jemand wohnt. Kein Fenster, keine Tuer mehr in Takt, nur Papierverklebung, wenn ueberhaupt das) und abgebrochen. Dafuer entstehen ueberall schon neue Wohnblocks, meist ziemlich hohe, weit useinanderstehend, fuer die bisherigen Slumbewohner – im Allg. Neger. Auch das Campusgelaende ist noch durchsetzt von Slumresten. Nicht mal die Haelfte des Gesamtplans ist bis jetzt verwirklicht, aber es geht enorm schnell voran. Seit Gus. hier ist, hat sich schon viel verbessert. Das Neueste fertige Gebaeude der Schule und wahrscheinlich auch das Schoenste bisher, ist die Architekturabteilung + Institute of Ind. Design. Es wurde erst Anfang des Jahres fertig. Vorher hausten die Architekten ziemlich provisorisch in einem andern Haus. Jetzt ist es ideal. Eine einstoeckige, ziemlich hohe Glashalle, ringsum von oben bis unten nur Glas. Ein fantastisches Licht im ganzen Raum, trotz der grossen Tiefe.

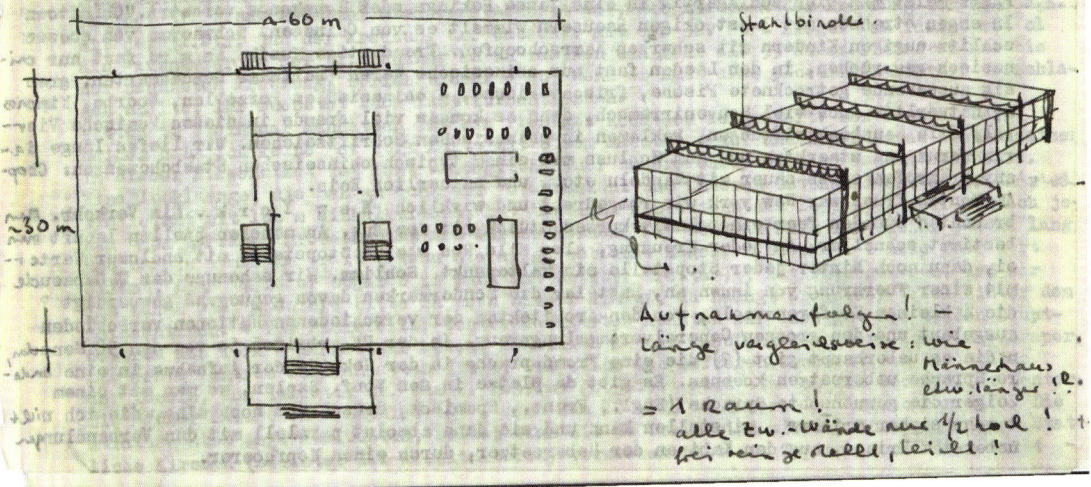

Original diary page with sketch of Crown Hall at IIT

locked in at these motorway stops, with fences all around. The drive went through endless fields, lots of corn fields, small woods in between, individual large groups of trees, then mostly the farms near them, with the typical, very cubic-looking barns (often painted dark red), a tall silo tower (round, with a shiny silver ball lid) and the residential house in old-fashioned English country house style, mostly two-storey, painted wood.

The drive into Chicago was great. First, you drive through all the heavy industries in the South, hideous-beautiful. Then, along the lake (Lake Shore Drive) into the centre. The city is built very stupidly. The most beautiful side, facing the lake, is reserved for cars. An eight-lane road along the entire shore, but mostly not close enough to properly see the lake. Wide strips of green on the right and left, park-like. Chicago is a huge city, insanely sprawling, mostly only two-to-three-storey buildings, with large stretches in between that are almost completely slummy, dilapidated and barely inhabited. Our IIT (Illinois Institute of Technology) is also in the middle of such a dilapidated area. They are currently in the process of tidying up the area in a long-term program. All the half-ruined, originally passable houses are being completely cleared out one after the other (sometimes you really wonder if anyone still lives in these holes, no windows, no doors intact, paper on the walls, if that) and demolished. On the other hand, new blocks of flats are already being built everywhere, mostly quite high, far apart, for the previous slum dwellers, generally Blacks. Even the campus area is still riddled with slum remnants. Not even half of the overall plan has been realised so far, but things are moving enormously fast. Since Günther has been here, a lot has already improved. The school's newest completed building (and probably the most beautiful so far) is the Architecture Department and the Institute of Design. It was finished only at the beginning of the year. Before that, the architects were living in a rather provisional building. Now it's ideal. A single-storey, relatively high, glass hall, all around from top to bottom all glass. Fantastic light in the whole room, despite the great depth.

One huge room, about 60 m by 30 m by 6 m high. Without any supports inside. Four steel trusses support the roof. The partitions drawn in the floor plan are all very light … and half-height (about 2.5 m) subdivisions made of wooden panel elements, natural oak or painted black or white – practical for pinning up the works currently on display, for small student exhibitions, etc. The space in the middle, separated from the main entrance, is the lobby, furnished with a few Barcelona armchairs, stools and low tables. This is where you go with guests for private conversations or if you want to sit comfortably for a while or take a nap or read something. Everything is so big, so spacious, that you can easily separate yourself everywhere. Toward the second entrance sit the two secretaries of the Architectural Department and the Institute of Design, each in their corner, almost 20 m apart. Otherwise, there are no secretaries in the whole thing. Everyone has two to three telephones, *c'est tous*. It works fantastically, with a minimal effort. The remaining partitions separate the individual classes a bit, on the right the Institute of Design people, on the left, the architects, with the undergraduates, in two shifts, and the graduates, split into people working on the thesis and those who aren't yet (like me, for example). Smaller enclosed rooms contain large drawing chests where everyone can keep all their stuff. Otherwise, you have a large drawing table outside, with plenty of space around it. The fantastic thing is that no one disturbs the other, although everything is in one pot. The room is so high, so plentiful, and the acoustic insulation is excellent (a freely suspended ceiling). In the basement are all the workshops, the toilets, for the 'ladies' for example, with its own relaxation room with couches, more cupboards (like in the T.H.), photo studios, a lounge-exhibition room where you can also play records, where the vending machines are for coffee, with or without milk, or cocoa, soup, beer – you only have to set a pointer, put in your money (the vending machine also changes money), and then you are 'automatically' poured what you want. Hot and fresh. During the first two weeks, nobody cared about us newcomers. We are about 10–15 newcomers in the graduate class. (In total, there are about 180 architects studying here, four of them girls. The majority are undergraduates. The rest are about 50 graduates, and I am the only girl). Three Americans, one Irishman, one Chilean, one Peruvian, two Germans (an Eiermann student), one Egyptian. Otherwise, there are Thai, Japanese, Indians, Siamese, etc. around us – almost all of them already have a degree, diploma, one or two masters, etc. The Irishman has worked for Corbusier in Paris for a long time. Most of the others have also had a lot of practice.

They say that our class is more advanced than average. So, in the first two to three weeks, we were left to muddle along on our own. The only hint, 'Design a house for Mies as you think it should be and for Hilbs design a city as you think it should be!' For Mies, this had to be done in ink on four mm thick illustration boards (that is miserable drawing paper mounted on thick, light cardboard, which is very expensive but completely unerasable. What you have to bear! Hilbersheimer was satisfied with less beautiful drawings.

After this 'entrance examination', which was then generally discussed and criticised – of course, no one was 100 per cent right – they then started with us anew. For Mies, we are now working on a courthouse (house with a courtyard, and mainly on a roughly 1/50 model). With Mies, the model is the most important thing. He works out everything himself in the model. Even the most important details are put together! It's great what comes to your mind in the process! What a difference in expression between the model and the drawing! Apart from that, of course, a fantastic model cult, everything of first-class materials that swallow up vast sums, even for such a small object.

Mies is at the school almost every day. How lucky we are! Last semester, it is said he was almost never there. He always comes in the afternoon. Then, he marches from table to table with his cane, criticises, discusses, or even says nothing. Sometimes, we sit together around a table, and there is a lot of silence. Now and then he says a few sentences, draws on a piece of paper to explain. We ask each other what's on their mind or something, and then we fall silent again. He often has the same thing to say over and over again. It's great. He doesn't try to keep on surprising, shining. What he teaches is clear, 'Forget your individualism … don't talk so much about functionalism, it's such a simple thing and an excuse.' All this is delivered in very bad English. Now and then he looks at me from the side, and then you usually get a German word thrown in (e.g. the other day when he criticised a detail and found it 'knitted', whereby no one could follow, he then said with a wink '*handgestrickt*' ('hand-made') we would say or some remark about Stuttgart, Weißenhof or something.

Hilbersheimer is a completely different type. Smaller, white-haired – he likes the students to treat him like one of their own. You can talk to him for hours about 'God and the world'. For him, we are currently working on floor plan types for social housing, with different living densities, bedroom types, etc. – sun diagrams. With him, all rooms have a south-east to south-west orientation.

Then, I took 'Special Problems' with Professor Peterhans, the third man in the group (former photography teacher at the Bauhaus, mathematician, philosopher (aesthetics)) – we work on space and other problems of line, surface, curvature in completely abstract ways. Here, too, everything is reduced to a minimum of effort and a maximum of effect and not without great difficulties! You must practice your form and sense of proportion enormously. At the same time, I'm taking English lessons. My English can take it. Every evening, from 5:00 to 6:00 p.m. Again, only five people in the class, two Italians, one Egyptian, one Chinese.

Here is a view of the Illinois Institute of Technology campus. Number 37 is the apartment building where I live, 31 is the cafeteria, bookstore, stationery shop, grocery store, hairdresser, post office, drug store, etc. The so-called student house (where we buy almost everything for our daily needs, because a trip downtown always costs two to three hours, it's all self-service shops, like almost everywhere here), 15 is the Architecture Department. At 1, 2, 3, etc. you can still see the old original buildings of the IIT, horrible red brick boxes that are gradually being completely demolished and replaced by new Mies houses. The Elevated Line runs through the middle of the campus, directly past the student home, known as the 'El' for short, Chicago's elevated and underground railway. It's a fabulous system that makes you wonder why accidents don't happen all the time. Downtown, it branches out in various directions, underground, with awful, dirty underground stations. Outside the city, it rattles through the area as an elevated train with a deafening noise. With the windows open, you can barely hear your own words as it speeds by. At first, I thought I'd never get used to it. Now, I sometimes can't hear it anymore (it's a good 150 m away, by the way). We're very close to the cafeteria, it's also open on Sundays, and there's breakfast, lunch, and dinner there as well as a running snack bar, of course, and the food is very lavish, i.e. for a ticket for an average of 85 cents per meal (varies for breakfast, lunch, and dinner), you can choose one of various salads, vegetables, and meats, have bread or toast, butter, milk as much as you want, a dessert, and coffee at the

end. By German standards, all these daily necessities are very lavish and relatively cheap (not, of course, when we start converting in the regular dollar-mark exchange rate). Food, clothes, shoes, and cars – and everything of fine quality and in the richest selection.
At least at first glance. As time goes by, you realise that there is only a very limited repertoire of food, for example, and the same everywhere. Steak, hamburgers, bacon, fried potatoes, rice, spaghetti and various sandwiches, vegetables all frozen, salads, ice creams, milkshakes, and not to forget the wonderful pies, which are fruit cakes, horribly sweet, sticky things, with horribly heavy, fat puff pastry. Biscuits, sweets, pralines, chocolate – all good but not quite very good. On the whole, I don't care about that. Besides, we cook almost everything ourselves – to finally finish the sentence I started above: although the cafeteria is very close, we almost never eat there. It costs too much money. Almost a dollar per meal, that's all we need for the whole day, almost. 'We' – I should explain that a bit more. You've probably all heard that I live with a Japanese woman. When I arrived here, I was already prepared to end up in a dormitory. Günther told me that all the girls of the IIT are housed in a dormitory (there are no more than 25) with an old lady in charge and everything. A better convent. Apart from feeling a bit too grown up, having to ask permission every time I leave the place, with bedtime at 10:00 p.m., etc., the thought of living together with 25 other females made my hair stand on end. But the individual flats are generally reserved for married students (every second student here has a wife and child), and the teaching and administrative staff. Occasionally, several students share a two-to-three-room flat, but that is rare and not welcome. That Günther has one alone is completely abnormal and was managed only with a lot of diplomacy and special connections – and he got it only a short time before I arrived. To make a long story short, I saw myself in the dorm. But, lo and behold, the graduate secretariat had automatically reserved a flat for me! Together with this Japanese woman. Probably because we are the only foreign graduate students (girls) at the whole IIT. Oh, I was happy. I arrived and was able to move right in, into a huge, spotlessly clean flat, with a cute bathroom and even cuter kitchenette, a big double closet, floor to ceiling. The furniture was all in a heap in the middle, it's not exactly the latest thing, it's a shame Mies had no say in

it – because the whole rest of the house is a Mies house, nine-storey, concrete skeleton (similar to a Promontory flat – also the upwardly receding supports, but windows all around, no end walls, that for experts) up to parapet height always sealed with yellow-grey clinker brick, steel windows above. The whole thing on supports. On the ground floor only two large, completely windowed halls, with a few armchairs and plants, a storage room for strollers, bicycles, children's toys, a room with the mailboxes (the second most important room in the building!), 90–100 flats – just as many mailboxes, and the two elevators, self-service, for approx. 8–10 people each. The stairs (two) inside are hardly used as such (only by me, the elevators are too slow for me), they are simple two-flight concrete platform stairs, enclosed, unplastered staircases, in which the garbage chutes, wastewater sinks, etc. are also located. Because there's no alternative, you shake out dirty rags, etc. in them, although it is, of course, forbidden, and if you have the usual vacuum cleaners and other machines, not necessary either. But we haven't got that far yet. In the basement, there are big storerooms, a ping-pong room, and the laundry room with machines for washing and drying, also soaking basins, etc. It costs 20 cents to use the machine once, you throw in soap powder and your laundry, and after 45 minutes the spin-dried laundry is ready. I usually forgo the drying, since it is so warm down there that everything dries by itself in an hour. So, you see, it's quite a feudal existence. The lifts often make me think of Auntie Maid! In our flat, too. Basically, it's like hers, as you can see in the sketch, except that everything is at least 1/3 bigger. There's a bathtub in the bathroom. The kitchen is not completely open to the room and is fully built-in. There is a closet for cleaning products, plenty of cupboards for dishes, a four-burner electric stove, a white-enamelled sink with running hot and cold water, lots of storage and working space. It's partly a kind of chopping board, make from raw wood (very practical), everything in the best finish, lots of chrome, white-lacquered aluminium sheet and, as the highlight, a gigantic icebox, also about 1/3 bigger than the Bosch, with a freezer compartment (indispensable for the many frozen things), huge ice boxes, various plastic inserts, etc. I wish you all had one of them.
The furniture consists of a strange sort of sofa-bed, from which you can pull out a second one, but we exchanged it for two very low, simple beds without any further

additions, a big linen chest that stands opposite the bathroom entrance, an even bigger pull-out table where we eat, with four chairs, a small desk that Reiko uses, a small club table, and a huge, upholstered armchair. Then there are bookshelves, to which we have added more, made of bricks and boards. I got a real drawing table from Günther, a hideous piece of furniture, but I'm glad of it. The parapet of our huge window (unfortunately facing north, with a broad view over low slums, almost uninhabited, partly already half demolished, at the very back the silhouette of the Loop (City) with the skyscrapers) is also on the inside in visible grey clinker brick. A large, stone-grey, thick cotton curtain closes all the windows in the house. Especially on the south side, practical for light regulation. Cork flooring, ceiling heating with thermostats, etc. make the whole thing complete, and although we couldn't exactly furnish ourselves nicely with the stupid furniture – and so get the urge to rearrange things every two weeks, which doesn't help much, because two people with two beds, two tables, etc. are just too much. Despite everything, we love our flat very much and are glad to have it. Reiko Hayashi, to introduce her to you by her full, euphonious name, is terribly nice. We liked each other, I think, from the very first moment. As I said, she studies industrial design, which is quite interesting for me to hear a bit about on the side. She seems to me to be an unusual example of the female part of her race and therefore has her own specific problems. Above all, she is afraid of returning home, though she wants to return to Japan via Europe next summer at the latest. We get on very well, and after a few adjustments at the beginning, I can't find anything 'foreign' about her now at all. We talk about everything and tell each other everything, often starting in the middle of the night and suddenly realising that it's already starting to dawn. At Christmas, I'll send some pictures of her. She has a lot of adorable kimonos with all the accessories, the little shoes, the funny pillows for the back, etc. You'll see. We keep a simple household. Whoever thinks it's necessary, and feels like it, does the shopping. We collect the receipts (with the appropriate name on the back), and it's all accounted for at the end of the month. Sometimes we cook together, sometimes not at all, sometimes we each cook for ourselves, whatever. Sometimes, we have guests together, then again 'privately'. I still have the advantage of being able to move into Günther's flat at any time, though lately it's not quite so easy since he stopped working at Skidmore and is at home more often. Still, it's sometimes nice to have a second room for a change. Günther is touching. He always lends me half his household, cooking pots, cleaning stuff, drawing stuff, his iron and ironing board have already completely ended up with us. Nevertheless, we still had enough 'purchases' ourselves, crockery, cutlery, glasses, towels, bed linen, etc. Money shouldn't actually be too tight for me, but with all the trappings, especially at the beginning, also with some debts at home (photo equipment, etc.), big expenses for all the drawing stuff, model building utensils (saws, files, welding torches, plexi-glass, metal profiles, wood, glues, veneers – fabulous!), all of it outrageously expensive, more dollars than marks! Book purchases, some clothing purchases, a winter coat was unavoidable in this icy wind here, and new shoes are still due. Plus, a hefty rent (each of us pays 45 dollars per month) plus telephone charges, you can't get by here without that.

Would you like to take down our number … 4845. I'm making a little money doing some drawing for the big bus company of America, Greyhound. Günther is my employer. We mainly have to draw maps, with the different lines. A hell of a fumble. Everything in ink on three mm thick white cardboard. Lots of lettering, with stencils or even better with foil paper letters. It's a great exercise in punctuality. And at the same time, I'm learning American geography.

After some initial difficulties, I received my money from the Soroptimists at the beginning of October for the whole first semester, i.e. the school fees (outrageously high, minimum fee per semester 375 dollars, English course is extra, I pay for that myself) are deducted and sent directly to IIT. I opened a savings account at the First National Bank of Chicago (Auntie Maid, is this company trustworthy?) and get money there when needed. For the time being, I seem to be getting by, but I could easily manage with double that, because, unfortunately, it's not as great as it sounds in Germany, 200 dollars per month = 800 DM. As I said, model stuff, flat, books … still. I don't know how interested you are in our daily stuff. I already have the feeling that I have gone into too much 'detail' and am boring you to no end. My daily routine? Very irregular. Normally, I get up between 7:30 and 8:30 a.m.. shower, do a bit of work until Reiko is ready. Generally, breakfast, plenty and together, eggs, ham, cornflakes, cream, fruit, juices (tomatoes, grapes, oranges, and pineapple), toast (from the oven, electricity is free), butter, jam, and honey. Are you amazed? But lunch is usually pretty much cancelled, at most a bit of fruit, a sandwich or a quick 'shake' in the canteen, around 2:00 p.m. I usually stay at home in the morning and work there. Around 1:00 to 2:00 p.m. off to school, lessons or work on the model, etc. until 5:00 p.m. Then, English class until 6:00 p.m. Go home, cook, whoever has more time and feels like it, sometimes the food is already ready when I get home, eat, rest a bit, and then, depending on whether I go to the Institute again (where it is particularly good to work in the evening, when it is almost empty), or work at home, or write letters, or read, or have visitors or do something. We almost never go out, especially me. Cinema, concerts, and theatre are almost completely out of the question, because there's not much going on. Rarely a lecture. Now and then a party, an invitation to a luncheon or dinner, from some club e.g. Institute of International Education, YWCA, Soroptimists. Our – my – 'private intercourse' is limited to a few students, mainly Hilda, a 32-year-old German (from Cologne), whose husband, an American, died in an accident three years ago, and who is now friends with an assistant at the Architecture Department (also German, from Aachen). Jan Lippert, a German Mies student, employed in the Mies office, two to three other German students or former students, Mitch – a Japanese industrial designer, Robin – an Irishman, Serge – a Chilean, Professor Peterhans – who lives in the same house and often visits or invites Reiko and me, he is the nicest and most interesting of all. We enjoy it a lot, and he has great books, pictures, and records. And, of course, Günther. More or less all my acquaintances ultimately come through him, or through Reiko, or through my class. Making more friends fails because of the lack of time – no need, too. What do you get out of it? I prefer to read something or stroll through the city, which is not really beautiful anywhere but is an inexhaustible treasure trove of the most curious observations. The Chinese quarter, with all its restaurants and shops, Italian, Japanese, Mexican quarters … German too, of course. There are shops where you think you are in Germany. Everything from there. Oetker's custard powder, Schwarzkopf shampoo, Rhine wines, 4711. At the 'Art Institute' there is an astonishing number of old and new acquaintances: Holbein, Rousseau, Beckmann, and Manet. There's also a fabulous art-book library where you can take any work ever written, from all over the world, out of the cupboard and browse as long as you like.

In mid-October, I took a trip to the country about 100 miles from Chicago. A small community invited us, a group of six foreign students (one doctor from Java, two Finns, two Englishmen, and me) for the weekend. We went out by train. Again, the same landscape as between New York and here. Single farms with huge fields. Now and then, a small village. We ended up in one of those. First impression:

15–20 villa-like, rather old-fashioned and somewhat romantic, English-looking wooden houses, loosely scattered in natural surroundings, with huge maple trees. No fence, hardly any kind of garden area. Just a road through the middle and a few paths branching off from it to the individual houses. Plus two churches, a general store, a post office, and the school, an old but very clean building. The children from the farms outside are collected by bus every morning. About two thirds live outside. The teacher and his … welcomed us at the station, where the train stopped especially for us, although the conductor couldn't believe what we were up to in the little nest. We were immediately loaded into two cars and drove to a forest picnic in the nearby 'community park'. This is a piece of forest that has been preserved as a place for excursions. One finds few real forests in this area. Woods are not interesting here. Only oil is used for heating. The afternoon was filled with various visits, to farms, the post office, etc. We were greeted by practically the whole village. The farms were particularly interesting for me. It seems almost unbelievable. Farms of about 100 acres are run by a single man, without any help, but with lots of livestock, cattle, cows, pigs, goats, etc. Towards evening, we were dropped off at individual families. I ended up in a very nice big house, far outside the village, actually already situated in the next community, Pecatonica. But they are not farmers, only renting a former farmhouse because they prefer to live outside town. The 'farmhouse' is good, by the way – a better two-storey villa on a small estate with many trees. The couple, about 35 years old with two children (Terry, a 14-year-old boy, Wendy, the 10-year-old spoilt daughter), and we took such a liking to each other that I have since visited them again twice. At Thanksgiving, together with Reiko, and now over New Year. It's really nice to have such a 'family' outside the city.

ACKNOWLEDGEMENTS

Thanks to Sibylle Schlaich for her emotional support and book design.
Thanks to Mike Schlaich for his emotional and financial support.
Thanks to Peter Schlaich, Brigitte's brother, for sharing childhood memories.
Thanks to Clara Schlaich, for her proofreading, clarifications,
and editorial suggestions.
Thanks to The International Archive of Women in Architecture for their financial
support and for serving as the catalyst for finishing this project.
Thanks to Sonia Cooke and Ursula Sobek for sharing their memories of Brigitte.
Thanks to my cousin Joseph Smith for translating Brigitte's diaries.
Thanks to Karen Widi, SOM Manager of Library, Records, and Information Services,
for coordinating the use of SOM project images.

ABBREVIATIONS

IIT – Illinois Institute of Technology
SOM – Skidmore, Owings & Merrill
BP – Brigitte Peterhans
Peterhans – Walter Peterhans

SOURCES

1. Blum, Betty J., *Oral History of Brigitte Peterhans*,
   (The Art Institute of Chicago, 2009)

2. Chang, Pao-Chi, and Swenson, Alfred,
   Architectural Education at IIT 1938 – 1978,
   (Illinois Institute of Technology, 1980)

3. Peterhans, Walter, as cited in *After Mies*,
   Werner Blaser, (Birkhauser Verlag, 1977)

4. Schlaich, Brigitte Eva, 'Students International House, Master Thesis',
   (Chicago: Illinois Institute of Technology, 1961)

5. Holgate, Alan, *The Art of Structural Engineering:
   The Work of Jörg Schlaich and His Team*,
   (Stuttgart: Edition Axel Menges, 1997)

6. Jones, Kristen, 'Visual Training at Illinois Institute of Technology:
   Aesthetics in Architectural Education, Doctor of Philosophy thesis',
   (Chicago: Illinois Institute of Technology, 2016)

7. Peterhans, Walter, 'Fragment on Aesthetics',
   Ratio, (Basil Blackwell, Vol. III, 1961)

8. Jones, Kristen, 'Visual', *Pioneering Women of American Architecture*,
   <http://www.pioneeringwomen.bwaf.org>

INDEX

People and Firms

Abshire, Nancy, 15
Adler, Dankmar, 8
Afshar, Ani, 15
Aicher-Scholl, Inge, 158
Allen, Davis, 31
Artigas, Josep Llorens, 33, 34, 102

Baker, Bruce, 25
Barr, Alfred Jr., 12
Barragan, Luis, 32
Beckmann, Max, 184
Behnisch, Guenter, 27, 32
Block, Mary, 60
Branczyk, Alexander, 152
Brandt, Marianne, 35
Braque, Georges, 102
Brenner Danforth Rockwell, 19
Brenner, Daniel, 31, 42
Brownson, Jacque, 13, 25
Burnham, Daniel, 8

Caldwell, Alfred, 18, 30, 40
Candela, Felix, 32
Cardinal Ratzinger, Pope Benedict, 14
Chang, Pao-Chi, 31, 72
Chryssa, 33
Coltrane, John, 21
Cooke, Sonia, 15
Corinth, Lovis, 35
Crane, Barbara, 32

De Blois, Natalie, 15, 31, 72
Draper and Kramer, 92

Faulkner, Willliam, 30
Fleener, David, 24, 25, 35

Giacometti, Alberto, 102
Godie, Lee, 20, 21, 33
Goldberg, Mayer, 20
Goldsmith, Myron, 13, 29, 31, 78
Graham, Bruce, 5, 17, 31, 34, 60, 66 102, 108
Graham, Jane Johnson, 31, 34, 60, 66
Graham, William, 34
Griffin, Walter Burley, 23
Gropius, Walter, 162

Hadid, Zaha, 25
Haid, David, 31
Hall, Edward T., 20
Hartman, William, 18, 34
Hayashi, Reiko, 182, 184
Heinle Wischer and Partners, 32
Hillberry, Susan, 23
Hilbersheimer, Ludwig, 13, 14, 30, 38, 178
Hitchcock, Richard, 12
Hitler, Adolph, 23
Hitler Youth, 27
Holabird and Root, 8
Holbein, Hans, 184

Itten, Johannes, 38

Jahn, Helmut, 32
Jenny, William Le Baron, 8
Johnson, Philip, 12

Kahn, Louis, 23
Kandinsky, Wassily, 38
Kerbis, Gertrude Lempp, 15, 19
Khan, Fazlur, 32, 78
Klee, Paul, 38

Laiblin, Dorothy, 26
League of German Girls (BDM), 27
Le Corbusier, 36, 177
Leonhardt, Fritz, 27, 32
Lewitt, Sol, 94
Lohan, Dirk, 14

Manet, Edouard, 184
Meyer-Waldeck, Wera, 161
Mies van der Rohe, Ludwig, 12, 13, 14, 16, 18, 29, 30, 33, 38, 39, 136, 158, 162, 163, 172, 178, 180, 184
Miro, Jean, 102

Nervi, Pier Luigi, 29
Netsch, Walter, 60
Nickel, Richard, 20, 23, 31
Norris, David, 19, 23, 24
Neutra, Richard, 12

Oh, Sae, 35
Otto, Frei, 27, 32

Pei, I. M., 24
Peterhans, Brigitte, 14, 15, 16, 18, 19, 20 21, 22, 24, 25, 26, 27, 28, 29, 30, 31, 32, 33, 38, 40, 42, 60, 66, 72, 76, 94, 102, 148, 160
Peterhans, Gesine Weise, 19
Peterhans, Julian Kerbis, 19
Peterhans, Michael, 19
Peterhans, Nini, 19
Peterhans, Walter, 13, 14, 18, 19, 20, 30, 31, 33, 35, 38, 39, 158, 179
Picasso, Pablo, 102

Reich Lily, 33
Rousseau, Henri, 184

Sander, Gunther, 20
Sandburg, Carl, 6
Sasaki, 32, 66, 78
Schindler, Rudolph, 12
Schlaich, Albert Eugen, 26
Schlaich, Anne, 27, 35
Schlaich, Christoph, 27
Schlaich, Clara, 27
Schlaich, Edith, 27
Schlaich, Elisabeth Weiss, 26

Schlaich, Eve Fezer, 27
Schlaich, Florian, 26, 35
Schlaich, Frieder, 27, 35, 152
Schlaich, Hans-Jacob, 27
Schlaich, Jörg, 15, 19, 27, 32, 34, 126, 136, 148, 154
Schlaich, Johannes, 27
Schlaich, Julie, 26
Schlaich, Katrin Grimm, 27
Schlaich, Kilian, 26
Schlaich, Klaus, 27
Schlaich, Konrad, 27
Schlaich, Ludwig, 26, 28, 122
Schlaich, Michael, 26
Schlaich, Mike, 19, 27, 35, 152, 154
Schlaich, Nikolaus, 26
Schlaich, Peter, 26, 35, 122
Schlaich, Sebastian, 26
Schlaich, Sibylle, 27, 103, 149, 152
Schlaich, Soenke, 27
Schneck, Adolph, 29

Schuette-Lihotzky, Margarite, 15
Schweiker, Paul, 25
Seidlein, Peter von, 32
Sharpe, David, 30
Simone, Nina, 21, 22
Siskind, Aaron, 30
Skidmore, Owings and Merrill, 13, 14, 18, 19, 22, 24, 25, 29, 31, 72, 76,78, 92, 94, 102, 106, 107, 108, 122, 136, 172, 182
Sobek, Ursula, 15
Soleri, Paolo, 23
Sommer, Frederick, 23
Sprague, Paul, 23
Sullivan, Louis, 8, 33

Taylor & Mathis, 94
Tomlinson, Richard, 16
Turner, Robert, 23, 24, 25

Ustinov, Peter, 26

Ustinov, Plato von, 26

Varnalis, Kozis, 25
Vaughn, Sarah, 21
Vinci, John, 15, 18, 30

Waters, Muddy, 21

Places

860 – 880 North Lake Shore Drive, Chicago, 13, 53
910 Lake Shore Drive, Chicago, 33, 37, 53

Aachen, Germany, 184
Ankara, Turkey, 30
Arab International Bank, 32, 86 – 91
Arcosante, 23
Armour Insitute of Technology, 13, 38
Artigas Foundation Studio, 102 – 107
Art Institute of Chicago, 21, 184
Auditorium Theater Building, 8
Atlanta, Georgia, 34

Bad Cannstatt, Germany, 27
Bauhaus, 14, 18, 30, 38, 39, 158, 162, 179
Baxter Travenol Corporate Campus, 32, 34, 78 – 85
Beijing, China, 24
Berlin, Germany, 27, 152, 154, 160
Berlin Building Exhibition of 1957, 162
Berliner Hochschule für Technik, 27
Bernese Oberland, Switzerland, 29
Bernloch, Germany, 28
Bietigheim-Bissingen, France, 28
Bonn, Germany, 161, 162, 163
Bremen, Germany, 163, 164
Broadgate Phase Eleven, 108 – 115

Cairo, Egypt, 32
Carson Pirie Scott Department Store, 8
Chartres Cathedral, 22
Chicago Building, The, 8, 11
Chicago Civic Center, 13
Chicago, Illinois, 8, 15, 19, 24, 25, 35, 158, 160, 171, 174, 176, 185
Chicago Plan, The, 8
Chicago School of Architecture, 8, 13
Chicago Stock Exchange, 8, 23

Chicago Symphony Orchestra, 21
Chicago Window, 8, 11
Chicago Women in Architecture Club, 15
Chillicothe, Missouri, 14
Cologne, Germany, 27, 184

Dhaka, Bangladesh, 23
Diakonie Kernen-Stetten, 118 – 121
Dresden, Germany, 162

Equitable Building, 72 – 75

Farnsworth House, 13
Frankfurt, Germany, 27, 172
Frieder Schlaich Residence, 154 – 157

Grand Canyon, 23

Hamburg, Germany, 27
Hamburg Art School, 31
Heilbron, Germany, 28
Home Insurance Building, 8, 9
Hong Kong, 23, 24
House for Her Parents, 122 –1 25

Illinois Institute of Technology, 13, 18, 19, 30, 31, 38, 42, 158, 160, 176, 180
Inland Steel Building, 13, 31, 60 – 65
Institute of Design, 19, 32 176, 177

Jin Mao Tower, 24
John Hancock Center, 13, 32
Joerg Schlaich Family Residence, 126 – 135

King Abdul Aziz International Airport, 14

Lake Michigan, 15
Lever House, 172
Lindau, Germany, 26
Long Island, New York, 167
Luxor, Egypt, 32

Madrid, Spain, 27
Marquette Building, 8
Max-Eyth-See Pedestrian Bridge, 148 – 151
Minneapolis, Minnesota, 33
Monadnock Building, 8, 10
Munich, Germany, 14
Munich Olympics, 27, 32
Museum of Modern Art, New York, 12
New River Gorge Bridge, 25
New York City, 160, 168, 170, 172, 174
New York Metropolitan Opera, 21

Orchestra Hall, Chicago, 8

Pleasant Hill Shaker Village, Kentucky, 24
Prairie Style, 8
Prescott, Arizona, 23

Reliance Building, 8
Roberts Show Lounge, Chicago, 21
Rockefeller Center, 170, 172
Rookery, The, 8
Rotesheim, Germany, 26

Schiller Theater, 8
Seagram Building, New York, 53, 173
Sears Tower, 13, 32, 76 – 77
Shanghai, China, 24
Sibylle Schlaich Residence, 152 – 153
Smart Museum of Art, Chicago, 35
SOM Offices, 92 – 93
Steinkopfstrasse Residence, Stuttgart, 136 – 147
Stetten, Germany, 26, 29, 36
Stuttgart, Germany, 15, 26, 27, 29, 32, 34, 160, 172
Sulz am Neckar, Germany, 26
Sutherland Hotel, Chicago, 21

Terraces at Perimeter Center, Atlanta, 34, 94 – 101
Tivoli Theater, Chicago, 21
Tuebingen University, 26

Ulm School of Design, 158
University of Bonn, 27
University of Chicago, 46, 47, 54, 158
University of Goettingen, 39
University of Stuttgart, 29, 31
Upjohn Corporate Headquarters, 31, 66 – 71

Virginia Polytechnic Institute, 24
Visual Training Course at IIT, 20

Wasmuth Portfolio, 12
Weishan, China, 24
Weissenhof Siedlung, Stuttgart, 136
Winona, Minnesota, 33

Zurich, Switzerland, 29

Brigitte on the Brooklyn Bridge _ Davis Allen

The Deutsche Bibliothek lists this publication in the Deutsche Nationalbibliografie; detailed bibliographic data is available on the internet at http://dnb.d-nb.de.

ISBN 978-3-86922-912-6

© 2025 by DOM publishers, Berlin
www.dom-publishers.com

This work is subject to copyright. All rights are reserved, whether the whole or part of the material is concerned, specifically the rights of translation, reprinting, recitation, broadcasting, reproduction on microfilms or in other ways, and storage or processing in data bases. Sources and owners of rights are given to the best of our knowledge; please inform us of any we may have omitted.

Copyediting
Sarah Roberts

Design
Moniteurs, Sibylle Schlaich

Printing
Druckhaus Sportflieger, Berlin
www.druckhaus-sportflieger.de